Table of Contents

Chapter	Page(s)
Dedication	2
Forward	3
How Uber Works	4-7
Ride Sharing Competition	8-10
Transporting Unaccompanied Minor (A must read for Passengers)	11-12
Driver Scams	13-14
Passenger Scams	15-17
Rating System (In and Outs)	18-21
Drivers	22-24
Passengers	25
People you may meet and Funny Stories	26-32
Uber Terms of Service	33-55
Lyft Terms of Service	56-84
Bibliography	85

Dedication

This book to dedicated first off to my family who has the patience to let me drive for Lyft and Uber. This includes my wife off 33 years Jenny, my son Brandon, my daughter Briana, and my Granddaughter Olivia Rose.

I also dedicate this book to all the drivers and passage that use the Uber and Lyft platform to make their lives and the lives of their family better. Without the passengers and drivers there is no ride sharing platforms.

My hat goes off to all of you that are responsible enough to not drink and drive and count on those drivers to get you home safely.

Forward

Lyft/Uber Survival Handbook ISBN: 9781793187109

As rideshare drivers we have certain expectation most of which is to earn a couple extra dollars. There are some things that may or may not happen that people never warn you about. Like the time the Adult film actress that tried to stick her tongue down my throat, or the angry passenger that gets upset because you won't start driving until they fasten their seat belt. How can anyone prepare you for that, truth is they can't.

As a rideshare driver I have met all kinds of people. I have met celebrities, actors, actresses, singers, Porn Stars, and yes even hookers. Between Uber and Lyft all the riders are different. I can only speak for myself but as an Uber driver I have never met celebrities, porn stars, or hookers, but I have met them through Lyft.

Remember to draw your line in the sand. Meaning the cars, you drive do not belong to Uber or Lyft they belong to you. Treat all your passengers with respect and they will reciprocate. The biggest thing is don't take crap from anyone and keep plugging away. You are not the passengers slave and do not have to do everything that they want like go through a drive though.

I wish all the drivers and passengers much success with using such an awesome service as ride share.

All the opinions listed here are not the expressed opinions of either Lyft or Uber. All the stories and situations within this book are 100 % true no matter how outlandish they may or may not sound.

All the information stated within may or may not work for everybody. Take Bruce Lee's old saying. **_"absorb what is useful and discard what is useless"_** . Meaning use what works for you as an individual or take what I am about to give you and develop it to fit your needs and situations.

Some information will be repeated as it pertains to both drivers and well as passengers.

You are probably wondering why did he put the terms and conditions in for both Lyft and Uber. Simple answer though, and it wasn't just to take up space. This lays out how drivers and passengers should act and behave. Remember we as drivers need to get you from point A to point B safely. We do have to follow the rules as set forth by the terms and conditions of the ridesharing companies.

I put the terms of Service for both Uber and Lyft all the way to back as I would hate to bore the hell out of everyone, but I thought that it would be nice for everyone to have just in case that a reference point is needed.

How Uber Ride Sharing Works

How to use the Uber app

Create an account

All you need is an email address and phone number. You can request a ride from your browser or from the Uber app. To download the app, go to the App Store or Google Play.

Enter your destination

Open the app and enter where you're going in the **Where to?** box. Tap to confirm your pickup location and tap **Confirm** again to be matched to a driver nearby.

Meet your driver

You can track their arrival on the map. When they're a few minutes away, wait for them at your pickup location.

Check your ride

For your personal safety, be certain that you're getting into the right car. Before hopping in, check the driver, car model, and license plate number against the information in the app. Once you're in the car, have your driver confirm your name before they go.

Sit back and relax

When you arrive, payment is easy. Depending on your region, you have options. Use cash or a payment method like a credit card or Uber Cash balance.

Rate your trip (Honestly)

Let them know how your trip went. You can also give your driver a compliment or add a tip in the app.

Leave a comment about your driver (Again Be Honest)

Let them know how you felt about your driver and your experience

Upfront pricing in real time

Before you confirm a trip, see price estimates so you don't have to guess and so you can compare costs to find the right ride, every time.

Perfect your pickup

When you request a ride, the app automatically suggests a convenient place to meet your driver. To adjust your location, just type in a new address or drag your pin on the map within the gray circle.

Adjusting your pick-up Location

Dropped your pin in the wrong spot? Put in the old address? Mistakes happen, which is why there's no need to cancel your ride. In order to adjust your pickup location. Simply edit your address and be on your way.

There's no need to cancel and re-request a pickup if you need to change your location. Edit your pickup address in the app and your driver will be with you shortly.

Get to know the person behind the wheel

Check Driver Profiles in the app to see fun facts about your driver, including ratings and compliments.

Get to know your drivers

Every driver has a story—and now you can find them in the Uber app. From compliments to ratings to fun facts, don't miss the opportunity to learn about the people who get you where you need

Hit the road faster with Saved Places

Your office. Your best friend's place. Your favorite coffee shop. These are places you go to time and time again. Save these addresses to your Uber app and get on your way a lot faster. Once you've saved a place, the option will be available as a shortcut every time you ride. With Saved Places, you'll be one tap away from where you want to be. Plus, it's easier than saving a contact to your phone. Finally, there's no need to remember the name or address of a place. Save it once and make it easier anytime you want to go there.

Send a ride for someone else

For times when you want to send your friends and family back home—or pick them up—you can request a ride for other adults through your app.

There's no need for them to have the app themselves. Simply request a pickup and Uber will text them important trip details.

Get more for your money with commuter benefits

You can now use eligible commuter benefits cards to pay for uberPOOL rides when you commute. This means you get more for your money by riding on pre-tax dollars. When paying with your commuter benefits card, you will be matched to a vehicle that seats 6 or more, which may lead to slightly higher wait times.

WHAT ARE COMMUTER BENEFITS?

Commuter benefits are employer-provided benefits programs that help employees save money on their monthly commuting expenses.

Employees of companies that provide commuter benefits programs can pay for public transportation—such as trains, subways, busses, ferries, or certain vanpools of 6 or more passengers—for their daily commute using pre-tax dollars. Funds are moved to a commuter account before taxes are deducted.

WHERE IS THIS PAYMENT OPTION AVAILABLE?

Currently, this option is available to uberPOOL riders in all US cities that offer uberPOOL. It is also currently available for ExpressPOOL riders in all cities that offer ExpressPOOL, except for San Diego and Atlanta.

WHAT IS UBERPOOL?

uberPOOL is our carpool option that matches you with riders heading in your direction so you can share your ride—and the cost. uberPOOL is always cheaper than uberX, up to 55% cheaper in some cities.

When you select uberPOOL, you'll be prompted to enter your destination. This can be an address, a venue name, or simply an intersection. We'll then show a guaranteed upfront fare before you request, so you'll always know what you're going to pay.

uberPOOL

Together, we save

uberPOOL matches you with riders heading in the same direction, so you can share the ride and cost.

- Affordable door-to-door rides
- Carpool with others in comfortable sedans
- Maximum 2 seats per request

Pool does take a little longer to get to your destination

With extra riders, it may take a little longer to get there, but you'll always see your estimated arrival time in the app. If you're in a rush, try uberX.

Limited riders within uberPOOL

Riders are only allowed to passengers per Pool ride. If you have more than that you will need to schedule an UberX instead.

In Conclusion

There is a lot to ride sharing to say the least. We have just scratched the service. Even though it seems over whelming at times on the do's and don'ts it's still a very simple mode of transportation if used correctly and within the ride sharing companies terms of service (TOS)

Ride Sharing Competition

Uber Technologies, the massive, omnipresent ride-sharing company, has dominated the industry since its inception in 2009. It has spread to more than 60 countries since then, and was recently valued at nearly $70 billion, making investors wonder when, and if, Uber will file for an IPO.

The emergence of on-demand rides has become a popular business venture all over the world, but it has proved difficult for companies to break away from the congested pack. At the end of 2015, Sidecar, another on-demand car service, officially stopped offering rides and deliveries.

If you're looking to leave controversy-plagued Uber behind-and recently, a lot of people did, rallying behind the #deleteUber hashtag after a certain executive order from President Trump, or after the drama of co-founder Travis Kalanick's resignation as CEO -but you still want the luxury of on-demand rides, there are increasingly popular alternatives for you.

Here's a rundown of the biggest competitors Uber faces:

Lyft

Launched in 2012, Lyft is a transportation company known for its fuzzy pink mustaches on the front or on dashboards of cars-silly, yet quite helpful when trying to spot your ride. In the U.S., Lyft is available in roughly 220 cities and areas nationwide, as well as nine cities within Indonesia, Malaysia, Singapore, Thailand, The Philippines, and Vietnam.

The San Francisco-based company works similarly to Uber. Within its smartphone app, users see a map with a pin at their location, animated cars moving around nearby, an estimate of how far away the nearest ride is, and a big button labeled "Request Lyft."

Lyft offers multiple levels of service: Lyft Line (a shared ride option that can save users up to 60% on fare); Plain Lyft (a ride for solo travelers or groups up to four); and Lyft Plus (larger cars and SUVs perfect for those traveling with suitcases and boxes, or if you want to ride with a large group). You can select which type of ride you want with a slider tool at the top of the app.

The ride-hailing company is also uniquely building a network of cars, focusing on autonomous vehicle technology. Lyft is working with General Motors GM -who is also an investor in the company-Alphabet's GOOGL self-driving car subsidiary Waymo, and most recently , self-driving car startup nuTonomy.

Curb

Formerly Taxi Magic (2009) and RideCharge (2007), Curb was born in 2014, and is a company that connects people with safe, reliable rides from professional, insured, and fully licensed taxi and other for-hire drivers. Based in Alexandria, Virginia, Curb operates in more than 60 U.S. cities nationwide, partnering with 90 cab companies and driving 35,000 cars.

Curb is app-based, opening up to a map that marks your location; it also shows available Curb drivers nearby. Users can either book rides instantly, or schedule them up to 24 hours in advance (a service convenient for travelers). There is a choice of paying fares within the app or with cash in the car, as well as vehicle options to best suit your needs.

On its website, Curb boasts that rides are always available and ready to pick you up, as well as messaging that "all rides begin and end at the curb," a motto reflected in its logo.

Didi Chuxing

Conceived from a merger back in 2015, Didi Chuxing is a ride-hailing service company made up of China's two largest taxi-hailing firms: Didi Dache and Kuaidi Dache. Didi Chuxing, formerly known as Didi Kuaidi, is often referred to as the "Uber of China," and virtually owns all of China's taxi-hailing market, with 99% market share, and 87% market share when it comes it hailing private vehicles.

It operates in over 400 cities across the region. The company said it booked 1.43 billion rides in 2015 alone, and completed 200 million rides last December. Didi is also in a strategic partnership with Lyft, which allowed the company to operate in China for the first time.

Didi Chuxing is well-funded and backed by tech giants Apple AAPL , Tencent Holdings TCEHY , and Alibaba BABA . According to its CrunchBase page, the company's total equity funding is valued at $12.94 billion in eight funding rounds from 21 investors.

Last year, Uber conceded defeat, selling its UberChina operations to Didi and ending an expensive, bruising battle between the two companies. Uber faced obstacle after obstacle trying to enter China's fast-growing ride-hailing market, losing a total of $2 billion there.

Grab

Founded in 2011, Grab (formerly known as GrabTaxi) is a ride service company that operates in Southeast Asia, primarily in Malaysia, Singapore, Thailand, Vietnam, Indonesia, and the Philippines. Like Uber, Grab works through an app-based platform for smartphones, and users can download the app on the Google Play store, Apple's App Store, and Blackberry World.

Grab has raised a total of $1.44 billion in total equity funding, with roughly 75,000 registered taxi drivers in its network.

Their mission is simple. Grab "aims to revamp these local taxi markets by introducing simple, cost effective mobile-based technology to both the supply (dispatch companies) and demand (passenger) sides of the distribution chain...[their] vision is to revamp the South East Asian taxi industry, making it a safer and more efficient means of transport we can all be proud of."

Announced last December, Grab joined in an alliance with Lyft, Didi, and Ola, India's main ride-hailing company, in order to compete with Uber as well as grow beyond its Southeast Asia market.

Ola

Started as an online cab aggregator in Mumbai back in 2010, Ola is an app-based transportation company and is one of the fastest growing businesses in India. It has raised $1.67 billion in equity funding through 10 rounds from 23 investors.

Ola currently has over 40,000 cars in its network across 22 cities.

Reserved through its mobile app, the company provides different types of cab services ranging from economic to luxury travel. Ola supports both cash and digital payment options with Ola money. It also recently rolled out two news services: outstation and rental. Outstation allows customers to book a cab two hours in advance for intercity travel, while rental lets customers rent a car on an hourly basis.

Like Lyft and Grab, Ola has partnered with Didi Chuxing in what is turning out to be quite the international effort against Uber. Together, the four companies rolled out joint products last year, beginning with Didi riders who, when visiting the U.S., can open their Didi app to hail a Lyft.

Driving Unaccompanied Minors

There is only one simple answer to picking up an unaccompanied minor. "DON'T DO IT". There are a few things that drivers should know.

1. Any passenger must be over the age of 18 to sign up or request a ride on either platform.
2. When canceling a ride on an unaccompanied minor Uber has a selection for why a driver is canceling a ride that states "Unaccompanied Minor".

There is a lot of responsibility for picking up a minor. They could be running away from home for all you know. They may or may not have their parents' permission to even leave the house. Bottom Line is that as a driver you don't know the situation and probably can't afford to get caught up in it.

Remember that if something goes wrong the driver can and will be held completely liable for the situation as an independent contractor to the Uber and Lyft platform. Also, if you are in violation of their terms of service you may not be covered under their insurance if you are in an accident. So, bottom line is doing the right thing and use common sense when transporting a passenger for a ride sharing company

Lyft's Policy:

Age requirement

Unaccompanied minors are prohibited from traveling with most carriers, Including TNC's. A passenger must be 18 to sign up for a Lyft account, but if a driver believes a passenger might be underage, the driver may ask the passenger to confirm their age. The driver may also let the passenger know that the driver will have to cancel the trip if the passenger is indeed under 18. In addition, drivers can report to transport unaccompanied minors by contacting support.

As a driver-partner, you should decline the ride request if you believe the person requesting the ride is under 18. When picking up riders, if you feel they are underage, you may request they provide a driver's license or ID card for confirmation. If a rider is underage, please do not start the trip or allow them to ride

Uber's Policy:

Requests from Underage Riders

As a driver-partner, you should decline the ride request if you believe the person requesting the ride is under 18. When picking up riders, if you feel they are underage, you may request they provide a driver's license or ID card for confirmation. If a rider is underage, please do not start the trip or allow them to ride.

Driver's Scams on Passenger's

1. **Faking an App Glitch.** Some riders have reported a driver announcing midway through the trip that their app has gone offline, which means they need to

receive payment in cash. After paying the driver, riders find their credit card on file has also been charged, meaning they have paid double, notes Jennifer McDermott, consumer advocate for personal finance website, finder.com. "A driver should never ask you to pay cash if you are traveling on a non-cash ride. Let them know you will not pay outside of the app, terminate the ride, and then report them if they insist or make you feel uncomfortable."

2. **Insisting you've selected cash.** In this scam, a driver will notify the rider on arrival at their destination that they (the rider) have selected a cash payment. The rider thinks they must have done so in error and pays the driver cash, only to be charged a cancellation fee due to the driver canceling just before arrival.

3. **Airport rides from non-Uber drivers.** At some airports like JFK, Harry many customers report random drivers trying to pick up riders who are waiting for their Uber and asking them to cancel the ride and just pay cash. "If you encounter this, it's most likely that you're not in an Uber and you should always prearrange the trips via the app,"

4. **Drivers scamming for cancellation fees.** If a rider tries to cancel a ride more than two minutes after requesting a ride, they are typically charged a cancellation fee. Some drivers will intentionally not drive towards the passenger in order to frustrate them and make them cancel, making the rider look at fault. "If you think this is happening, just send a note to Uber through the help tab of the passenger app. You can always request a refund of your cancellation fee from the trip tab on the menu and explain what happened,"

5. **Asking you to pay tolls.** Nope. "Any tolls incurred during a trip will be automatically charged by Uber to the rider and then paid back to the driver. Some drivers may try to scam you for tolls but others just may not know how the tolls process works as Uber doesn't provide much training to drivers for these situations," Remember that while en route, there are no additional charges or out-of-pocket expenses, ever. If your driver requests cash, simply don't pay.

6. **Bait-and-switch scams.** In this one, a ride share is summoned, the driver accepts, then cancels, and a driver shows up, in a different car, saying he's not the same driver (but after you are en route). It is likely that the driver was the original, but in a different vehicle and he or she ultimately charges cash as much as twice the fee. Prior to disembarking, always confirm the fee and confirm the destination. If there is a discrepancy, simply cancel immediately and summon another driver."

7. **The trip doesn't end when you get out of the car.** In response to any additional charges, go into the app, and report your concerns to the company to flush out any potentially fraudulent charges.

8. **Charging a fake "cleaning fee".** Be wary that if you're with a loud big group, you are a good candidate for an extra "cleaning fee" that can be added after your ride ends. "Some unethical drivers aren't shy about communicating vandalization if they didn't like their client. "A $35 ride can turn into a $150 one, thanks to the

added fee. If you feel like the driver isn't happy with your party, and you're wary the situation could generate into added fees, take pictures of the inside of the vehicle before you leave. This way you can challenge the fee immediately."

9. **Re-requesting the Uber ride.** Before you re-request a ride due to a malfunction on the app, as a driver may claim, ask to view their app and check your own app, because re-requesting a ride bumps the fare by 35 percent due to surge pricing. "This is a little trick some drivers try to get a higher fare. Don't comply with their friendly demand until you are sure there was an error in the system.

These are just to name a few. There are a few more but these are the major scams that the unethical drivers try to pull. Just be careful and use your common sense. If you think that you are being taken advantage of by the driver, go ahead and report them. This may not solve your issue but they at least know that if their activity won't be tolerated.

Passenger Scams on Driver's

1. **Impersonating an Uber or Lyft employee to ask for your password.** The first one is the most easy to recognize, and that's impersonating an Uber or Lyft

employee. There are a couple of variations of this. This first one is that you'll receive a request and then as soon as you accept it you'll get a phone call from someone claiming to be an employee. They'll say that it's an identity verification and they'll ask for your Uber or Lyft password. Obviously, you should never give anyone your password and Uber and Lyft would never want to ask you for it. This is just an attempt to get into your account, take your money. Another variation of this is is that someone will take a ride from you and they will claim that you will not be getting paid through the app, you'll be getting paid through some other way. I've heard of them giving pretty legit looking business cards and claiming that you have to give Uber this code and then they'll pay you a bunch of extra money or something. Obviously, it's fraud.

2. **Two types of ride theft for passengers and drivers.** There are two variations of ride theft you should know about. The first is a 'passenger stealer' ride. This is especially common in very metropolitan areas during the downtown rush hours. This is why you never want to ask, "Are you Kenneth?" You instead say, "What's your name?" Or you'll ask, "What's the name associated with the account?" You also don't want them to see your phone because they may look at the name and then tell you that's their name. Another one is a driver stealing a ride from another driver. The other driver may or may not actually be an Uber driver. What they'll do is they'll pick up the passenger and the passenger doesn't actually care if they're in the right Uber. They just tell them where they're going, maybe give them cash. But a lot of times they'll see a passenger waiting and then they'll claim that there was something wrong with the app and request to be paid in cash and Venmo or requesting a ride separately.

3. **Bringing too many passengers for the ride type.** If you're in an area that has Uber Pool or Lyft Line, sometimes people will request a ride but they will not disclose how many people they're bringing with them. Pool and Line have a maximum of two people that you can bring with them. Any more than that, you need to request the whole car. The other one is bringing more than they requested. For example, if they request an Uber X, which only allow five passengers and then you driving your Uber XL arrive, they'll put in more. Or they'll just try to squeeze additional people than there are seat belts. If you have an Uber XL, you can request that they adjust the payment and they usually will. But if you have an Uber X and you take six people in your five passenger car, it will adjust it and you could risk getting in trouble, both with the law and with the companies. If they tell you they will give you a great tip for it, never believe them. Anything someone says about a tip is a lie

4. Passengers asking drivers to take a different route or go to a different destination. **Sometimes a passenger will ask you to go a different direction instead of following the GPS and then that will drive up the price. At which point they will claim to the company that you did that yourself and then they'll be reimbursed for the ride and you'll lose out on it. They may also ask for a different drop-off location and do the same thing.**
5. **Anchoring during stops.** Sometimes passengers will request stops and being a nice person, you may or may not allow them. Being the savvy driver you are, you of course tell them to keep it under three minutes if possible and they say, "Yes, of course. No problem." But they leave their bag in the car or their dog or their baby. I'm not even kidding. I've had drivers tell me that. Then when they're gone for 25 minutes, you can't just leave. Or you can and you can just drop it off at your hub or I don't know, fire department if it's a baby.
6. **Surge fraud.** Sometimes a passenger will be smart enough to realize that where they're being picked up is surging, so they will change the pick-up location to an area that's not surging. They will then call up the driver and say, "Hey, I'm actually not at where the pick-up is and I don't know how to change it. Can you pick me up at the corner of this and this?" Now they get a ride that starts where they want without paying the surge pricing. Never pick someone up at a different location than what's in the app. Anything that you do that's not following what the app says is a risk for you. Go to the pick-up location, wait, cancel.
7. **Lying about the driver A.K.A. "Put your driver on blast".** There's this photo that's floating around that gives you different ways to put your driver on blast to get a free ride. One example is to take trash from your bag, put it on the ground, take a photo, send that to Uber or Lyft, claiming that the car is dirty and getting reimbursed. People who do any of these things are terrible, but these ones are the worst, in my opinion. You can literally be deactivated for things on that list. You could be ruining someone's livelihood.

8. **Canceling mid-ride.** This one is increasingly common. By canceling the ride they can no longer rate them and the driver is no longer getting paid for that ride. If that happens, you should literally just let them out. Some people will do it right on the freeway, personally I would get to an exit first, but yeah, get that person

out of your car. If someone cancels a ride, you are no longer protected by the apps or your insurance and you also are not getting paid, so get them out.

Now, the biggest thing that you can do to protect yourself from these kinds of scams is have a dash cam. Preferably one that faces both inward and outward. The one that I have and has a lot of great reviews is the Vantrue Pro2. It records both in and out and has good night vision.

Another thing that you can do is keep your sound on for your phone to make sure that you know is someone has canceled, especially if you use a different app for navigation.

And the last thing is don't rely on just one program. If you drive for Uber, drive for Lyft as well so that if you get canceled on Uber then you still have Lyft as a backup, especially if you rely on it for paying your bills.

Hopefully this was helpful and now you know some ways to protect yourself. If you appreciate the things that I'm doing,

The Famous Rating System

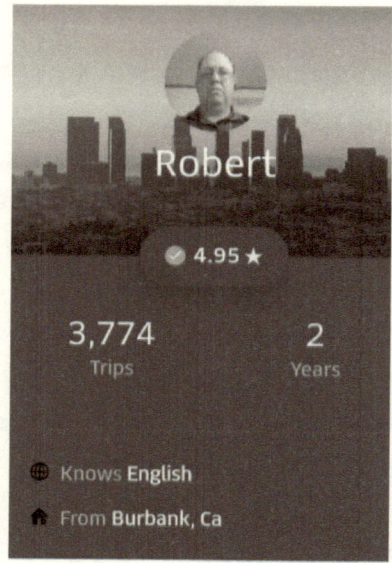

The rating system is a 5-star point system that applies to both drivers and passengers. Some passengers are not aware of the fact that the drivers rate them as well. As you can see in the above picture I as a driver has a 4.95-star rating with almost 4,000 rides and 2 years of service with Uber. In this section I will explain how a passenger or driver can get a low rating. Also, I will talk about how to keep you rating high. We will also delve into the impact of having a low rating.

Low rating explained

Below is a list of items that will cause passengers to give a low rating to a driver. Some may seem petty and they are, but these are the reasons riders may rate a driver low.

Drivers List

- Dirty Vehicle (Inside or Out)
- Loud Music
- Music not Loud Enough
- Wrong Genre of Music
- Talking too Much
- Not Talking Enough
- Taking a Phone Call During a ride
- Language Using Sexual Content
- The Use of Profanity
- Car Smells of Cigarette Smoke or Marijuana.
- Cologne is to Strong

- Bad Breath
- Talking Poorly about Their Significant Other
- Personal Hygiene
- Not Following GPS
- Following GPS and its wrong
- Traffic
- Talking about Religion
- Talking about Politics
- Not Taking the Passengers Route
- Not Making Stops as Passenger Requests ie: Drive Through

The list for drivers could go on forever. Seems ridiculous and petty on some of the items on the list, right? These are the reason though that drivers get a low rating. The list below for passengers is much shorter, because we as drivers have a lot more to deal with. The drivers are also not as picky about the passengers as they are about the drivers. I have also seen passengers flat out lie about the driver to the ridesharing company to get them in trouble. We will talk about that later in the book.

Passengers List

- Taking a Phone Call During a ride in a Pool with Other Passengers in the Car
- Talking about Religion
- Talking about Politics
- Personal Hygiene
- Talking too Much
- Not Talking Enough
- The Use of Profanity
- Smells of Cigarette Smoke or Marijuana
- Aggressive Behavior (Bullying)
- Intoxicated
- Giving Directions
- Feeling entitled
- Disrespecting Driver
- Being Rude
- Talking Down to the Driver
- Leaving Trash in the Car
- Leaving Items in The Car ie: Cell Phone
- Not Tipping
- Making the driver wait for a while

The passenger list is also a long list. I was as complete as possible but I am sure there is more to add to this list. A lot of them also seem very petty but this is the reality of it. You can't please everyone and you will send people off the edge for the smallest of things. The items in red are some of my personal pet peeves that I have an issue with.

An example of how I received a low rating from a passenger is. one day I picked up a couple going to lunch I was asked "Do You Have an Aux Cord". They wanted to play music. I said flat out "I don't allow RAP to be played in this car. One of the riders looked at me and said "Are you serious" I said "Absolutely". I didn't do what they asked so they rated me low. Take into consideration it was less than a 5-minute ride. The passengers must remember the cars do not belong to Uber or Lyft they are the driver's personal vehicles and should be respected as such.

I have another story to share that happened when I first started driving in October of 2015. This was when I was driving strictly for Lyft. When a passenger would rate a driver, they could also leave a comment about that driver. I took these very personally. Some are very nice but some are downright vicious. Earlier I spoke about passengers lying about the drivers and this was the case. I picked up this couple heading to a club. The woman asked me "Can you put some music on" I said "Of Course I Can". I completed the ride with no issues and then at the end of the week I got her feedback. She had said things like "He didn't turn up the music as loud as I wanted" "He was listening to our conversation, which I didn't appreciate" This was not true. She blasted me too Lyft anyway.

Here is a statement to all the passengers. "Communicate". If the driver is talking to much **LET THEM KNOW.** If the music is to loud or to soft **LET THEM KNOW.** The thing is when you report us me trivial items to make us look bad then you as the passenger is messing with our income and this could affect our wellbeing and our family. I am not saying that you should never report a driver, but just make sure it is worth reporting. Like if a driver was inappropriate with their language or actions then by all means report them, but don't report them for the music being too soft like that person did to me.

Drivers have the risk of being deactivated if their rating reaches 4.6 stars or lower. I believe that passengers should have to meet the same standards. The star rating is import for riders for this reason. If I am driving at 3 or 4 AM and I get a ride request for a rider with a 4.6-star rating I will not be picking them up, due to their low rating. I would imagine that it works the same for drivers.

Funny thing about ratings is a low rating may not be the person's fault. Here are some examples of no fault low ratings (Traffic, GPS Navigation, Other Passengers acting up). When a passenger gives a driver a low rating the passenger is given options of why the low rating. Well Uber has put a program in place if someone gives the driver a low rating and the reason is completely out of the drivers control then the low rating doesn't count against the driver.

If a passenger lets a friend use their App to get home and the friend acts the fool that could affect that passengers rating. I have met some very nice people with low ratings.

Let me assure you that not everyone is guilty of everything on this list, and some don't do any of these things. This is a list of the most common things that people do to get lower than a 5-Star Rating from a driver or passenger.

In the next couple of sections, we will discuss how passengers and drivers should act towards one another. This will keep your rating very high

Drivers

Drivers are the core of the ridesharing community weather they drive for Lyft, Uber, or both. If it wasn't for drivers there would be no Uber or Lyft. We will be discussing the trials and tribulations of being a driver in today's markets.

As drivers, we will get all kinds of passengers and each one needs to be handled a little differently. The worst ones that I have encountered are those who have entitlement issues. Don't let them get to you they are few and far between. Remember though I am from Los Angeles and this is the entitlement capitol of the world. This is exactly the reason that I don't like to pick-up in Beverly Hills because of all the pretentious people that reside there. The only thing that I can say is that knowing your passengers will take time, you will say some stupid things just dust yourself off and move on. If you drive for Lyft do not take the negative comments to heart like I did.

Your passengers may lie to the companies about you or something they said you did, but really didn't. If you have an issue with a passenger, and I mean any issue please do yourself a favor and let the company know right away. You have no idea what they will do or say to you, and this is part of lively hood. You need to watch your back. Passengers will lie just to get a discount or a free ride and they will screw you to do it. There is only one person that will have your back always and that's you. Watch your back and always do the right thing.

How do the drivers keep that 5-star rating? Here are some things that may be quite helpful and very easy to follow and maintain,

- Keep the vehicle clean inside and out. We are all busy and I realize that can be difficult at times to maintain the cleanliness of your vehicle.
- Always be nice
- Know you passengers. Meaning know when to talk to them and when not to.
- Do not use any profanity
- Don't talk religion or politics
- Do not under any circumstances breach the topic of sex or use sexual innuendos
- Spray your vehicle with Fabreeze or some air freshener prior to every shift.
- Also, have an air freshener in your car like that one that mounts to the air vents
- Honor passenger's requests within reason and at your discretion. Remembering it's your time and your car.

Some passengers are just hard to please and never give a 5-star anything. But these tips will hell. I right now am maintaining a 4.95 which is great for a driver of over 2 years.

Drivers are human no matter what people think, and as human's errors can be made either in judgement of verbiage. There has been a talk for a while about Uber coming out with driverless cars. **WOW REALLY!** The only thing this will do is put more money into the giant companies, because they won't have to split the profits with a human. There is no interacting with another person. I personally don't think it's going to go anywhere. I would not trust a driverless car to get me to my destination safely.

With that said let's talk about drivers. How should drivers act? That is really a great question. Take into consideration that we are human and some of us are not as young as we used to be.

First thing that drives need to find out that patience is truly a virtue. 95% of the time the riders will not be out front waiting to get in their car. When a rider orders a car what typically happens is the passenger lives on the 38th floor of a 39-floor building and is not even ready to walk out the door. This is where the driver's patience comes into play. The riders are aware at least with Uber they will not be charged waiting time for two minutes after the driver arrives. So typically the passenger will show up at 1 minute and 59 seconds, but as drivers we remain calm and patient. This is a pet peeve of mine and I get why drivers will give a low rating over something like making them wait.

When can, a driver refuse a service dog? NEVER!!!!!!!!!!! If a passenger gets in the car with a service dog, you must except that ride or suffer possible deactivation for breaking the law. This includes all service animals including animals for emotional support, physical support, mental support, or for the sight challenged individuals. I love animals so all dogs are welcome. I get only mildly perturbed if someone has a dog that is not a service animal and I don't get that courtesy call asking if that would be ok with me. Other than that, I welcome them all.

As a responsible driver, please don't take advantage of customers as listed in the drivers scamming passengers section of this book. Drivers need to be honest, and have integrity about them. They should try to lengthen the ride to jack up the fare, because that is theft if it's done maliciously.

What should you do if a passenger refuses to get out of your car once you canceled the ride for not connecting with the rider and upon cancelling the rider shows up. What can you do? You can ask them to leave, that doesn't work. Your only next step is to go to the app to have Uber call the police. You passenger is now trespassing. If you call 911 from your phone odds are the call will go to your state highway patrol like it does in California. Can you go hands on and physically remove them? I would let the police take of it. If you go hands on you may find yourself in the grey bar motel (Jail) for the night on a battery charge. Please don't let that happen.

Also, If you smoke marijuana, for goodness sake don't do it in the car. If someone has been smoking pot gets in your car as a passenger, when they leave spray your car with air freshener. You know how many times I have had to explain that I am not a pot smoker, because my last passengers stunk up the car. If you do smoke it don't get behind the will high. It's still a DUI even if pot was made legal by your state. Don't consume alcohol and drive for Uber of Lyft. As rideshare drives the Blood Alcohol Content (BAC) is cut in half, for example the normal BAC in

California is .08 but as a rideshare driver it's .04. Don't chance it, if you do drink, stay home where's it's safe. It's your responsibility to support your family and make it home in one piece.

I personally have given about 7000 rides between Uber and Lyft and have never had someone violent or someone who threw up in my car. Even when that Uber driver got beat up by that taco bell executive the driver sort of antagonized him. Not saying the driver had that beating coming, but he could have handled it differently and with more tact.

Bottom Line to all the current and future drivers, be kind, be courteous, be patient, be understanding, a good listener, and part psychologist and you'll be fine. Remember to follow the Terms of Service of the ridesharing companies that you are doing work for.

Get a dash cam. A dash cam is going to be a very valuable tool. It will tell a story if a ride goes south. Please check all your local laws about using a dash cam. In California, there must be a sign posted telling the passengers that they will be on camera and audio. Best type of camera will be a double facing camera to view your inside and out in case you are in an accident as well.

Main thing is to all the drivers is be safe, drive carefully, and don't take crap from anyone. There is a lot more I can go in about carrying weapons ie: knives, pepper spray, etc. Check your local laws and use common sense.

Almost forgot a couple things. Most drivers like to talk, and passengers do to. If you start talking to your passengers and they are answering you in one word response, then stop talking they don't want to. Don't risk a low rating cause to can't shut up.

Boy this section was longer than I had wanted to make it.

Passengers

As a passenger, you love the convenience of calling a car to take you where you want to go quickly and for a great price right? There is a lot more to ride sharing then people realize. This will be a lot shorter than the driver section.

One thing all passengers must remember is that the car that they are getting into belongs to the driver. It's not owned Lyft or Uber. So all of your requests will be up to the drivers discretion, and if he won't fill your request try not to be upset.

There are a lot of drivers that aren't exactly the nicest people out there, just deal with it for the deration of the ride and pay them back when you rate them. With that said, If you get in the car with a driver that has a 4.6 star rating don't be surprised that they aren't a nice person. There is a reason that they have a low rating.

Drivers rate passenger just like passenger's rate drivers. Here are some things that could help you maintain a 5-star rating.

- Be outside and waiting when the driver arrives. (don't order the car until you are ready)
- Do not make a lot of requests of the driver especially unreasonable ones.
- Do not leave your trash in their car
- Do not leave personal items behind like your cell phone, wallet, etc.
- Be nice to your driver
- Do not treat the driver like a second-class citizen and your personal chauffer.
- Don't be entitle. We drive you from point A to point B. We don't have to go through a drive-through just because you want us to.
- Give directions only when asked. There is nothing more irritating to the driver when he has a GPS and the passenger insists on giving directions.
- If you have smoked pot prior to your ride and still stink of that pot smell. The best thing to do is own up to it and immediately apologize to the driver. They will appreciate it.

Bottom line is being nice and think about it this way. If I was a driver what would I not like? Then as a passenger do the opposite.

If a driver asks you to get out of his vehicle for whatever reason, do yourself a favor and exit the vehicle. If he asks you to exit the vehicle and you refuse, then you are trespassing. If the police are summoned there may be more trouble, then you want to deal with. After all who wants to spend the night in jail.

People you may meet and Funny Stories

As a driver, I have met all kinds of people including celebrities, producers, directors, teachers, porn stars, and yes even prostitutes, and there are stories that go with them.

One celebrity that I picked up (Not mentioning any names) but they were on a very popular network sit-com. Very nice person and we became good friends, and I still don't know how that happened. Anyway, I thought that their head was so big that the car was going to tip over.

Seldom do drives and passengers see each other more than once I guess I am one of the lucky ones. I pick this actress up a couple times. She is the lead on a Net Flix show the 100's. She was the loveliest and nicest person I have ever had the opportunity of meet. I was lucky with this one she was just sweet.

I have met actors from the Thundermens, GLOW, Awkward, and many more. I have been very luck in that a aspect. All the big names that I have met have always been extremely nice.

One night I even drove a husband and wife that were the founder of a group called Group Love, they were just about to open the Hollywood Bowl for a group called Imagine Dragons. I called my 20-year-old daughter while they were in the car and she went nuts. My daughter thought that I was cool for about a second.

There are also things that happen that may seem a little odd and nothing like what happened will ever happen again. One night I picked up a nice young lady at Burbank Airport and I drove her to an address in Highland Park. Well, I decided to turn off my App and head pack to the Airport. I picked up a nice couple. We started driving and I noticed that their address was also in Highland Park just like my previous passenger. It turned out I dropped this couple to the exact same address as my previous passenger. If I lived to be 150 years old that will probably never happen to me again.

One morning early I picked up this girl that was 20 something and she was wearing PJ's. She gets in and I ask what she did for work and right away she told me she was an adult actress, and then she crawled in to the front seat. It was a short right and she was high and drunk. I was ending the ride and when I parked she tried to stick her tongue down my throat. That was a little wild but I stopped it immediately, and went on with my day.

One early morning about 4:00 A.M. I picked up a gentleman that had been partying a little and he was of an alternative life style. The ride ended and he was out of the car. Thank god, the ride had ended, because real casually he said I think that I should tip you with a hand job or blowjob. I was shocked to say the least. I said nothing, he closed the, and I went on my way

These aren't the half of the stories that I could share. They are just at the top of the list. I hope to have many more on my next addition.

The New Year's Eve Surprise

On New Year's Eve 2015, Edmonton, Alberta resident Matthew Lindsay and four friends were leaving a wedding in Mill Woods. They opted for an Uber ride (fact: Uber is currently illegal in Edmonton). Sure, they were notified that surge pricing was in effect, at least for the first stop they made (not the subsequent two), but didn't think it would be THIS bad. The damage? $1,114.75.

After discussion with Uber, which claims they inform all users of all surge pricing via push notifications, the company and Lindsay agreed to a partial refund - Uber offered him $500.

The Belligerent Bro

Not all ridesharing horror stories involve nefarious drivers. Sometimes, it the passengers themselves who. Such was the case in Costa Mesa, California in October of 2015, when one wasted, backwards hat-wearing dude assaulted his Uber driver after being asked to get out of the cab.

Uber driver Edward Caban caught the whole violent ordeal on his dashboard cam. He told police that the passenger, 32-year-old Benjamin Golden, was so drunk that he couldn't give accurate directions home and was acting aggressively toward Caban. The driver eventually pulled over in a parking lot and demanded that the drunk idiot get out of his car. But Golden refused, springing on Caban, punching him, pulling his hair, and trying to slam his head into the window. Caban managed to get out his pepper spray and let Golden have it.

Golden, a brand manager for Taco Bell, was arrested on a misdemeanor charge and fired from his job after video of the assault went viral. He was also banned from ever using Uber again. Caban says he will no longer drive for the ridesharing company either, since he's had too many run-ins with belligerent, obnoxious, and apparently dangerous bros like Golden.

The Shooter

On June 1, 2018, Denver police say an Uber driver shot and killed his passenger after an argument. The shooting occurred around 2:45 am.

"There appears to be a conflict between an Uber driver and his passenger. The passenger did suffer gunshot wounds or wounds and was transported to the hospital where subsequently he was pronounced dead a short time later," officer Sonny Jackson

The driver, Michael A. Hancock, was handcuffed on site and later arrested for investigation of first-degree murder. Police officers found a semiautomatic Ruger SR 40 tucked in Hancock's waistband.

The Strangler

In September of 2013, Bridgett Todd was choked by her Uber driver. The incident was an apparent racist attack on the woman, though Uber's CEO was outraged that they could be to blame for it.

The Snapper

Olivia Nuzzi of The Daily Beast once had an Uber driver who, upon entering his vehicle, showed her a picture he had snapped of her earlier in the day while walking on the street. While this Uber horror story is enough to stop anyone from using the service again, Nuzzi later encountered another driver who admitted to seeing her Facebook profile picture before and wanted to know whether or not she was single.

The Kalamazoo Killer

Michigan Uber driver Jason Brian Dalton was charged with six counts of murder for a rideshare-assisted in February, 2016. Dalton was accused of driving from one target to another, shooting people at random, and picking up and dropping off Uber riders between shootings.

Authorities say he shot a woman in the parking lot of an apartment complex, then shot and killed a father and son outside a car dealership, and finished his spree by shooting five people in the parking lot of a Cracker Barrel restaurant, killing four and gravely wounding a 14-year-old girl. Remarkably, he continued driving people around, including one person who took an Uber as an alternative to walking while an active shooter was on the loose - only to wind up in Dalton's car. The rider took the ride having no idea he was in the alleged shooter's car, and wasn't harmed.

Dalton was arrested without incident in downtown Kalamazoo, with no apparent motive to the killing spree, or connection to the victims.

The Five Star

It's human nature to want to be liked, but some people take it too far. This was the case with one Uber driver, who allegedly locked his passenger in his car and demanded that she give him a five-star rating. When they first arrived at her destination, the driver locked the doors, turned around, and asked her to see her phone to see how much the ride had cost. She showed him, but then he tried to grab the phone and said he would not let her leave until she gave him the best rating. Finally, she did, and only then did he let her leave.

The Stalker

So many rideshare horror stories involve unwanted sexual advances. After taking a Lyft, one woman was repeatedly texted by her driver, asking her to hang out. Although she politely declined, this did not stop his persistence.

The Chicago Rapist

A Washington woman called an Uber after leaving a bar with some friends. The woman claims that when she was in the car, the driver kept making advances towards her, which she ignored. But when she got out of the car, the driver apparently got out as well, grabbed her from behind, knocked her to the ground, and raped her. The driver was charged with first degree sexual assault

The Sidecar Predator

After partying with her friends, one woman took a sidecar home. But once they were a couple of blocks away from her destination, the driver told her that she had the "sexiest voice" he had ever heard and suggested instead of taking her home, they go somewhere to talk. She demanded he let her out. Fortunately, he did, and her boyfriend came to pick her up

Self-Driving Car Disaster

On March 18, 2018 in Tempe, Arizona, a involving a self driving Uber car. Around 10 PM, 49-year-old Elaine Herzberg was crossing the street at a busy intersection. A self-driving Uber car struck Herzberg and she later died of her injuries. While the car was in autonomous mode, there was a driver behind the wheel. Uber's autonomous vehicle pilot program was suspended briefly after a non-fatal crash involving a self-driving car in December 2016.

The Killer

In perhaps one of the most tragic and saddest rideshare horror stories to date, Uber driver Syed Muzaffar was arrested for vehicular manslaughter when he struck and killed a six-year-old girl on New Year's Eve. The event happened in San Francisco, and Uber is now facing a wrongful death suit, as it never researched the reckless driving charges the driver had incurred several years before.

The Kidnapper

After a club bouncer called an Uber for an intoxicated 26-year-old woman in LA, the lady woke up in a hotel hours later, and she wasn't alone. Next to her was her Uber driver, Frederick Dencer – shirtless. The driver was later charged with kidnapping.

The Burper

Sometimes our bodily functions just escape us. But on February 13, 2012, Seth Bender had no idea his burping in his Uber would result in the driver ranting and screaming about how much he hates Americans and homosexuals. When Bender and his friend exited the car, the driver then proceeded to spit in his face and slap him. It's not like Bender didn't excuse himself after burping – he said he did.

The Criminal

When calling an Uber in New Orleans, Hannah Jegart assumed she would be taken right home. What she didn't anticipate is that – mid-ride – her driver would be arrested. Apparently, in the middle of the ride, a "plain-clothed" officer ripped open the driver's door to arrest him. Not only was she suddenly left without a ride home, but it was raining too

The Two Hour Detour

Most residents of big cities know that they need to be careful of cab drivers taking long routes home on purpose, hoping to run the meter higher. But after a night out partying with her friends, one woman took an LA Uber home, only to have the driver ride around for two hours, finally stopping in an empty parking lot with the doors locked. He only agreed to take her home after she began screaming and yelling at him.

The Fondler

Knowing whether to sit in the back or the front can be a debate for some. But one Uber taker quickly learned her lesson when her Chicago driver asked her to sit in the front, then began fondling her once she did. Later, the driver was charged with a misdemeanor battery

The Hammer

26-year-old Uber driver Patrick Karajah was arrested for assault with a deadly weapon and battery with serious bodily injury after attacking his passenger with a hammer in San Francisco. After picking up a group of friends from a bar at 2am, Karajah and one of the male passengers got into a fight about the route he was taking. Karajah pulled over, forced the man to get out of the car, then hit him with a hammer and drove away.

The Racist Criminal

San Francisco UberX driver Daveea Whitmore was not happy when his passenger, a 28-year-old man named James Alva attempted to take photos of Whitmore and his car's license plate. Whitmore allegedly called Alva a "dirty Mexican f----t" and hit him several times. Despite the fact that Uber claims to run background checks on their drivers, Whitmore had "at least one felony conviction involving prison time" for marijuana sales. This, despite Uber's "zero-tolerance" policy for drug offenses.

The Delhi Rapist

Terrifying ride share stories don't just take place in the USA. With Uber's expansion across the globe, there have been even more troubling tales from countries like India, where a driver was accused of raping one of his passengers.

Even more troubling, the driver, 32-year-old Shiv Kumar Yadav was a career criminal who was out on bail for sexually assaulting a woman. In fact, he had a history of shady behavior and had been arrested for other crimes like robbery, molestation and possessing an unlicensed firearm.

The Getaway Driver

Passengers looking to get home quickly will never complain about their slow drivers after a story like this. Ryan Simonetti claims his Uber driver took him and two colleagues on a "high speed chase" in Washington, D.C. Simonetti driver began to get nervous after he noticed that taxi inspector was following the car.

At one point, the driver told his passengers, "I'm sorry, we're going to have to run this red light." He proceeded to drive well above the speed limit, dodging other cars and refusing to slow down. After 8-10 minutes, Simonetti and his friends were released from the car, but their driver fled into Virginia.

The Price of Safety

This horror story doesn't involve Uber's drivers as much as it does their insane "algorithmic" pricing policies. When a hostage crisis took over a neighborhood in Sydney, Australia, nearby civilians had good reason to want to catch a ride away from the danger zone. But because demand spiked so rapidly, so did prices. Uber charged fleeing Australians fares upwards of $100 to escape the area.

Uber Terms of Service (TOS)

U.S. Terms of Use

Effective: December 13, 2017

1. Contractual Relationship

These Terms of Use ("Terms") govern your access or use, from within the United States and its territories and possessions, of the applications, websites, content, products, and services (the "Services," as more fully defined below in Section 3) made available in the United States and its territories and possessions by Uber USA, LLC and its parents, subsidiaries, representatives, affiliates, officers and directors (collectively, "Uber"). PLEASE READ THESE TERMS CAREFULLY, AS THEY CONSTITUTE A LEGAL AGREEMENT BETWEEN YOU AND UBER. In these Terms, the words "including" and "include" mean "including, but not limited to."

By accessing or using the Services, you confirm your agreement to be bound by these Terms. If you do not agree to these Terms, you may not access or use the Services. These Terms expressly supersede prior agreements or arrangements with you. Uber may immediately terminate these Terms or any Services with respect to you, or generally cease offering or deny access to the Services or any portion thereof, at any time for any reason.

IMPORTANT: PLEASE REVIEW THE ARBITRATION AGREEMENT SET FORTH BELOW CAREFULLY, AS IT WILL REQUIRE YOU TO RESOLVE DISPUTES WITH UBER ON AN INDIVIDUAL BASIS THROUGH FINAL AND BINDING ARBITRATION. BY ENTERING THIS AGREEMENT, YOU EXPRESSLY ACKNOWLEDGE THAT YOU HAVE READ AND UNDERSTAND ALL OF THE TERMS OF

THIS AGREEMENT AND HAVE TAKEN TIME TO CONSIDER THE CONSEQUENCES OF THIS IMPORTANT DECISION.

Supplemental terms may apply to certain Services, such as policies for a particular event, program, activity or promotion, and such supplemental terms will be disclosed to you in separate region-specific disclosures (e.g., a particular city webpage on Uber.com) or in connection with the applicable Service(s). Supplemental terms are in addition to, and shall be deemed a part of, the Terms for the purposes of the applicable Service(s). Supplemental terms shall prevail over these Terms in the event of a conflict with respect to the applicable Services.

Uber may amend the Terms from time to time. Amendments will be effective upon Uber's posting of such updated Terms at this location or in the amended policies or supplemental terms on the applicable Service(s). Your continued access or use of the Services after such posting confirms your consent to be bound by the Terms, as amended. If Uber changes these Terms after the date you first agreed to the Terms (or to any subsequent changes to these Terms), you may reject any such change by providing Uber written notice of such rejection within 30 days of the date such change became effective, as indicated in the "Effective" date above. This written notice must be provided either (a) by mail or hand delivery to our registered agent for service of process, c/o Uber USA, LLC (the name and current contact information for the registered agent in each state are available online here), or (b) by email from the email address associated with your Account to: change-dr@uber.com. In order to be effective, the notice must include your full name and clearly indicate your intent to reject changes to these Terms. By rejecting changes, you are agreeing that you will continue to be bound by the provisions of these Terms as of the date you first agreed to the Terms (or to any subsequent changes to these Terms).

Uber's collection and use of personal information in connection with the Services is described in Uber's Privacy Statements located at www.uber.com/legal/privacy.

2. Arbitration Agreement

By agreeing to the Terms, you agree that you are required to resolve any claim that you may have against Uber on an individual basis in arbitration, as set forth in this Arbitration Agreement. This will preclude you from bringing any class, collective, or representative action against Uber, and also preclude you from participating in or recovering relief under any current or future class, collective, consolidated, or representative action brought against Uber by someone else.

Agreement to Binding Arbitration Between You and Uber.

You and Uber agree that any dispute, claim or controversy arising out of or relating to (a) these Terms or the existence, breach, termination, enforcement, interpretation or validity thereof, or (b) your access to or use of the Services at any time, whether before or after the date you agreed to the Terms, will be settled by binding arbitration between you and Uber, and not in a court of law.

You acknowledge and agree that you and Uber are each waiving the right to a trial by jury or to participate as a plaintiff or class member in any purported class action or representative proceeding. Unless both you and Uber otherwise agree in writing, any arbitration will be conducted only on an individual basis and not in a class, collective, consolidated, or representative proceeding. However, you and Uber each retain the right to bring an individual action in small claims court and the right to seek injunctive or other equitable relief in a court of competent jurisdiction to prevent the actual or threatened infringement, misappropriation or violation of a party's copyrights, trademarks, trade secrets, patents or other intellectual property rights.

Rules and Governing Law.

The arbitration will be administered by the American Arbitration Association ("AAA") in accordance with the AAA's Consumer Arbitration Rules and the Supplementary Procedures for Consumer Related Disputes (the "AAA Rules") then in effect, except as modified by this Arbitration Agreement. The AAA Rules are available at www.adr.org/arb_med or by calling the AAA at 1-800-778-7879.

The parties agree that the arbitrator ("Arbitrator"), and not any federal, state, or local court or agency, shall have exclusive authority to resolve any disputes relating to the interpretation, applicability, enforceability or formation of this Arbitration Agreement, including any claim that all or any part of this Arbitration Agreement is void or voidable. The Arbitrator shall also be responsible for determining all threshold arbitrability issues, including issues relating to whether the Terms are unconscionable or illusory and any defense to arbitration, including waiver, delay, laches, or estoppel.

Notwithstanding any choice of law or other provision in the Terms, the parties agree and acknowledge that this Arbitration Agreement evidences a transaction involving interstate commerce and that the Federal Arbitration Act, 9 U.S.C. § 1 et seq. ("FAA"), will govern its interpretation and enforcement and proceedings pursuant thereto. It is the intent of the parties that the FAA and AAA Rules shall preempt all state laws to the fullest extent permitted by law. If the FAA and AAA Rules are found to not apply to any issue that arises under this Arbitration Agreement or the enforcement thereof, then that issue shall be resolved under the laws of the state of California.

Process.

A party who desires to initiate arbitration must provide the other party with a written Demand for Arbitration as specified in the AAA Rules. (The AAA provides a form Demand for Arbitration - Consumer Arbitration Rules at www.adr.org or by calling the AAA at 1-800-778-7879). The Arbitrator will be either (1) a retired judge or (2) an attorney specifically licensed to practice law in the state of California and will be selected by the parties from the AAA's roster of consumer dispute arbitrators. If the parties are unable to agree upon an Arbitrator within seven (7) days of delivery of the Demand for Arbitration, then the AAA will appoint the Arbitrator in accordance with the AAA Rules.

Location and Procedure.

Unless you and Uber otherwise agree, the arbitration will be conducted in the county where you reside. If your claim does not exceed $10,000, then the arbitration will be conducted solely on the basis of documents you and Uber submit to the Arbitrator, unless you request a hearing or the Arbitrator determines that a hearing is necessary. If your claim exceeds $10,000, your right to a hearing will be determined by the AAA Rules. Subject to the AAA Rules, the Arbitrator will have the discretion to direct a reasonable exchange of information by the parties, consistent with the expedited nature of the arbitration.

Arbitrator's Decision.

The Arbitrator will render an award within the time frame specified in the AAA Rules. Judgment on the arbitration award may be entered in any court having competent jurisdiction to do so. The Arbitrator may award declaratory or injunctive relief only in favor of the claimant and only to the extent necessary to provide relief warranted by the claimant's individual claim. An Arbitrator's decision shall be final and binding on all parties. An Arbitrator's decision and judgment thereon shall have no precedential or collateral estoppel effect. If you prevail in arbitration you will be entitled to an award of attorneys' fees and expenses, to the extent provided under applicable law. Uber will not seek, and hereby waives all rights Uber may have under applicable law to recover, attorneys' fees and expenses if Uber prevails in arbitration.

Fees.

Your responsibility to pay any AAA filing, administrative and arbitrator fees will be solely as set forth in the AAA Rules. However, if your claim for damages does not exceed $75,000, Uber will pay all such fees, unless the Arbitrator finds that either the substance of your claim or the relief sought in your Demand for Arbitration was frivolous or was brought for an improper purpose (as measured by the standards set forth in Federal Rule of Civil Procedure 11(b)).

Changes.

Notwithstanding the provisions in Section I above, regarding consent to be bound by amendments to these Terms, if Uber changes this Arbitration Agreement after the date you first agreed to the Terms (or to any subsequent changes to the Terms), you may reject any such change by providing Uber written notice of such rejection within 30 days of the date such change became effective, as indicated in the "Effective" date above. This written notice must be provided either (a) by mail or hand delivery to our registered agent for service of process, c/o Uber USA, LLC (the name and current contact information for the registered agent in each state are available online here), or (b) by email from the email address associated with your Account to: change-dr@uber.com. In order to be effective, the notice must include your full name and clearly indicate your intent to reject changes to this Arbitration Agreement. By rejecting changes, you are agreeing that you will arbitrate any dispute between you and Uber in accordance with the provisions of this Arbitration Agreement as of the date you first agreed to the Terms (or to any subsequent changes to the Terms).

Severability and Survival.

If any portion of this Arbitration Agreement is found to be unenforceable or unlawful for any reason, (1) the unenforceable or unlawful provision shall be severed from these Terms; (2) severance of the unenforceable or unlawful provision shall have no impact whatsoever on the remainder of the Arbitration Agreement or the parties' ability to compel arbitration of any remaining claims on an individual basis pursuant to the Arbitration Agreement; and (3) to the extent that any claims must therefore proceed on a class, collective, consolidated, or representative basis, such claims must be litigated in a civil court of competent jurisdiction and not in arbitration, and the parties agree that litigation of those claims shall be stayed pending the outcome of any individual claims in arbitration.

3. The Services

The Services comprise mobile applications and related services (each, an "Application"), which enable users to arrange and schedule transportation, logistics and/or delivery services and/or to purchase certain goods, including with third party providers of such services and goods under agreement with Uber or certain of Uber's affiliates ("Third Party Providers"). In certain instances the Services may also include an option to receive transportation, logistics and/or delivery services for an upfront price, subject to acceptance by the respective Third Party Providers. Unless otherwise agreed by Uber in a separate written agreement with you, the Services are made available solely for your personal, noncommercial use. YOU ACKNOWLEDGE THAT YOUR ABILITY TO OBTAIN TRANSPORTATION, LOGISTICS AND/OR DELIVERY SERVICES THROUGH THE USE OF THE SERVICES DOES NOT ESTABLISH UBER AS A PROVIDER OF TRANSPORTATION, LOGISTICS OR DELIVERY SERVICES OR AS A TRANSPORTATION CARRIER.

License.

Subject to your compliance with these Terms, Uber grants you a limited, non-exclusive, non-sublicensable, revocable, non-transferable license to: (i) access and use the Applications on your personal device solely in connection with your use of the Services; and (ii) access and use any content, information and related materials that may be made available through the Services, in each case solely for your personal, noncommercial use. Any rights not expressly granted herein are reserved by Uber and Uber's licensors.

Restrictions.

You may not: (i) remove any copyright, trademark or other proprietary notices from any portion of the Services; (ii) reproduce, modify, prepare derivative works based upon, distribute, license, lease, sell, resell, transfer, publicly display, publicly perform, transmit, stream, broadcast or otherwise exploit the Services except as expressly permitted by Uber; (iii) decompile, reverse engineer or disassemble the Services except as may be permitted by applicable law; (iv) link to, mirror or frame any portion of the Services; (v) cause or launch any programs or scripts for the purpose of scraping, indexing, surveying, or otherwise data mining any portion of the Services or unduly burdening or hindering the operation and/or functionality of any aspect of the Services; or (vi) attempt to gain unauthorized access to or impair any aspect of the Services or its related systems or networks.

Provision of the Services.

You acknowledge that portions of the Services may be made available under Uber's various brands or request options associated with transportation or logistics, including the transportation request brands currently referred to as "Uber," "uberX," "uberXL," "UberBLACK," "UberSELECT," "UberSUV" and "UberLUX" and the logistics request products currently referred to as "UberRUSH," and "UberEATS." You also acknowledge that the Services may be made available under such brands or request options by or in connection with: (i) certain of Uber's subsidiaries and affiliates; or (ii) independent Third Party Providers, including Transportation Network Company drivers, Transportation Charter Permit holders or holders of similar transportation permits, authorizations or licenses.

Third Party Services and Content.

The Services may be made available or accessed in connection with third party services and content (including advertising) that Uber does not control. You acknowledge that different terms of use and privacy policies may apply to your use of such third party services and content. Uber does not endorse such third party services and content and in no event shall Uber be responsible or liable for any products or services of such third party providers. Additionally, Apple Inc., Google, Inc., Microsoft Corporation or BlackBerry Limited will be a third-party beneficiary to this contract if you access the Services using Applications developed for Apple iOS, Android, Microsoft Windows, or Blackberry-powered mobile devices, respectively. These third party beneficiaries are not parties to this contract and are not responsible for the provision or support of the Services in any manner. Your access to the Services using these devices is subject to terms set forth in the applicable third party beneficiary's terms of service.

Ownership.

The Services and all rights therein are and shall remain Uber's property or the property of Uber's licensors. Neither these Terms nor your use of the Services convey or grant to you any rights: (i) in or related to the Services except for the limited license granted above; or (ii) to use or reference in any manner Uber's company names, logos, product and service names, trademarks or services marks or those of Uber's licensors.

4. Access and Use of the Services

User Accounts.

In order to use most aspects of the Services, you must register for and maintain an active personal user Services account ("Account"). You must be at least 18 years of age, or the age of legal majority in your jurisdiction (if different than 18), to obtain an Account, unless a specific Service permits otherwise. Account registration requires you to submit to Uber certain personal information, such as your name, address, mobile phone number and age, as well as at least one valid payment method supported by Uber. You agree to maintain accurate, complete, and up-to-date information in your Account. Your failure to maintain accurate, complete, and up-to-date Account information, including having an invalid or expired payment method on file, may result in your inability to access or use the Services. You are responsible for all activity that occurs under your Account, and you agree to maintain the security and secrecy of your Account username and password at all times. Unless otherwise permitted by Uber in writing, you may only possess one Account.

User Requirements and Conduct.

The Service is not available for use by persons under the age of 18. You may not authorize third parties to use your Account, and you may not allow persons under the age of 18 to receive transportation or logistics services from Third Party Providers unless they are accompanied by you. You may not assign or otherwise transfer your Account to any other person or entity. You agree to comply with all applicable laws when accessing or using the Services, and you may only access or use the Services for lawful purposes (e.g., no transport of unlawful or hazardous materials). You may not in your access or use of the Services cause nuisance, annoyance, inconvenience, or property damage, whether to the Third Party Provider or any other party. In certain instances you may be asked to provide proof of identity or other method of identity verification to access or use the Services, and you agree that you may be denied access to or use of the Services if you refuse to provide proof of identity or other method of identity verification.

Text Messaging and Telephone Calls.

You agree that Uber may contact you by telephone or text messages (including by an automatic telephone dialing system) at any of the phone numbers provided by you or on your behalf in connection with an Uber account, including for marketing purposes. You understand that you are not required to provide this consent as a condition of purchasing any property, goods or services. You also understand that you may opt out of receiving text messages from Uber at any time, either by texting the word "STOP" to 89203 using the mobile device that is receiving the messages, or by contacting help.uber.com. If you do not choose to opt out, Uber may contact you as outlined in its User Privacy Statement, located at www.uber.com/legal/privacy.

User Provided Content.

Uber may, in Uber's sole discretion, permit you from time to time to submit, upload, publish or otherwise make available to Uber through the Services textual, audio, and/or visual content and information, including commentary and feedback related to the Services, initiation of support requests, and submission of entries for competitions and promotions ("User Content"). Any User Content provided by you remains your property. However, by providing User Content to Uber, you grant Uber a worldwide, perpetual, irrevocable, transferable, royalty-free license, with the right to sublicense, to use, copy, modify, create derivative works of, distribute, publicly display, publicly perform, and otherwise exploit in any manner such User Content in all formats and distribution channels now known or hereafter devised (including in connection with the Services and Uber's business and on third-party sites and services), without further notice to or consent from you, and without the requirement of payment to you or any other person or entity.

You represent and warrant that: (i) you either are the sole and exclusive owner of all User Content or you have all rights, licenses, consents and releases necessary to grant Uber the license to the User Content as set forth above; and (ii) neither the User Content, nor your submission, uploading, publishing or otherwise making available of such User Content, nor Uber's use of the User Content as permitted herein will infringe, misappropriate or violate a third party's intellectual property or proprietary rights, or rights of publicity or privacy, or result in the violation of any applicable law or regulation.

You agree to not provide User Content that is defamatory, libelous, hateful, violent, obscene, pornographic, unlawful, or otherwise offensive, as determined by Uber in its sole discretion, whether or not such material may be protected by law. Uber may, but shall not be obligated to, review, monitor, or remove User Content, at Uber's sole discretion and at any time and for any reason, without notice to you.

Network Access and Devices.

You are responsible for obtaining the data network access necessary to use the Services. Your mobile network's data and messaging rates and fees may apply if you access or use the Services from your device. You are responsible for acquiring and updating compatible hardware or devices necessary to access and use the Services and Applications and any updates thereto. Uber does not guarantee that the Services, or any portion thereof, will function on any particular hardware or devices. In addition, the Services may be subject to malfunctions and delays inherent in the use of the Internet and electronic communications.

5. Payment

You understand that use of the Services may result in charges to you for the services or goods you receive ("Charges"). Uber will receive and/or enable your payment of the applicable Charges for services or goods obtained through your use of the Services. Charges will be inclusive of applicable taxes where required by law. Charges may include other applicable fees, tolls, and/or surcharges including a booking fee, municipal tolls, airport surcharges or processing fees for split payments. Please visit www.uber.com/cities for further information on your particular location.

All Charges and payments will be enabled by Uber using the preferred payment method designated in your Account, after which you will receive a receipt by email. If your primary Account payment method is determined to be expired, invalid or otherwise not able to be charged, you agree that Uber may use a secondary payment method in your Account, if available. Charges paid by you are final and non-refundable, unless otherwise determined by Uber.

As between you and Uber, Uber reserves the right to establish, remove and/or revise Charges for any or all services or goods obtained through the use of the Services at any time in Uber's sole discretion. Further, you acknowledge and agree that Charges applicable in certain geographical areas may increase substantially during times of high demand. Uber will use reasonable efforts to inform you of Charges that may apply, provided that you will be responsible for Charges incurred under your Account regardless of your awareness of such Charges or the amounts thereof. Uber may from time to time provide certain users with promotional offers and discounts that may result in different amounts charged for the same or similar services or goods obtained through the use of the Services, and you agree that such promotional offers and discounts, unless also made available to you, shall have no bearing on your use of the Services or the Charges applied to you. You may elect to cancel your request for Services at any time prior to the commencement of such Services, in which case you may be charged a cancellation fee on a Third Party Provider's behalf. After you have received services or goods obtained through the Service, you will have the opportunity to rate your experience and leave additional feedback. Uber may use the proceeds of any Charges for any purpose, subject to any payment obligations it has agreed to with any Third Party Providers or other third parties.

In certain cases, with respect to Third Party Providers, Charges you incur will be owed directly to Third Party Providers, and Uber will collect payment of those charges from you, on the Third Party Provider's behalf as their limited payment collection agent, and payment of the Charges shall be considered the same as payment made directly by you to the Third Party Provider. In such cases, you retain the right to request lower Charges from a Third Party Provider for services or goods received by you from such Third Party Provider at the time you receive such services or goods, and Charges you incur will be owed to the Third Party Provider. Uber will respond accordingly to any request from a Third Party Provider to modify the Charges for a particular service or good. This payment structure is intended to fully compensate a Third Party Provider, if applicable, for the services or goods obtained in connection with your use of the Services. In all other cases, Charges you incur will be owed and paid directly to Uber or its affiliates, where Uber is solely liable for any obligations to Third Party Providers. In such cases, you retain the right to request lower Charges from Uber for services or goods received by you from a Third Party Provider at the time you receive such services or goods, and Uber will respond accordingly to any request from you to modify the Charges for a particular service or good. Except with respect to taxicab transportation services requested through the Application, Uber does not designate any portion of your payment as a tip or gratuity to a Third Party Provider. Any representation by Uber (on Uber's website, in the Application, or in Uber's marketing materials) to the effect that tipping is "voluntary," "not required," and/or "included" in the payments you make for services or goods provided is not intended to suggest that Uber provides any additional amounts, beyond those described above, to a Third Party Provider you may use. You understand and agree that, while you are free to provide additional payment as a gratuity to any Third Party Provider who provides you with services or goods obtained through the Service, you are under no obligation to do so. Gratuities are voluntary.

Repair, Cleaning or Lost and Found Fees.

You shall be responsible for the cost of repair for damage to, or necessary cleaning of, vehicles and property resulting from use of the Services under your Account in excess of normal "wear and tear" damages and necessary cleaning ("Repair or Cleaning"). In the event that a Repair or Cleaning request is verified by Uber in Uber's reasonable discretion, Uber reserves the right to facilitate payment for the reasonable cost of such Repair or Cleaning using your payment method designated in your Account. Such amounts, as well as those pertaining to lost and found goods, will be transferred by Uber to a Third Party Provider, if applicable, and are non-refundable.

The amounts related to repair, cleaning or lost & found fees applicable in Puerto Rico may be found at https://www.uber.com/es-US/blog/puerto-rico/puerto-rico-terminos-y-condiciones/ and may be updated from time to time solely by Uber.

6. Disclaimers; Limitation of Liability; Indemnity.

DISCLAIMER.

THE SERVICES ARE PROVIDED "AS IS" AND "AS AVAILABLE." UBER DISCLAIMS ALL REPRESENTATIONS AND WARRANTIES, EXPRESS, IMPLIED, OR STATUTORY, NOT EXPRESSLY SET OUT IN THESE TERMS, INCLUDING THE IMPLIED WARRANTIES OF MERCHANTABILITY, FITNESS FOR A PARTICULAR PURPOSE AND NON-INFRINGEMENT. IN ADDITION, UBER MAKES NO REPRESENTATION, WARRANTY, OR GUARANTEE REGARDING THE RELIABILITY, TIMELINESS, QUALITY, SUITABILITY, OR AVAILABILITY OF THE SERVICES OR ANY SERVICES OR GOODS REQUESTED THROUGH THE USE OF THE SERVICES, OR THAT THE SERVICES WILL BE UNINTERRUPTED OR ERROR-FREE. UBER DOES NOT GUARANTEE THE QUALITY, SUITABILITY, SAFETY OR ABILITY OF THIRD PARTY PROVIDERS. YOU AGREE THAT THE ENTIRE RISK ARISING OUT OF YOUR USE OF THE SERVICES, AND ANY SERVICE OR GOOD REQUESTED IN CONNECTION THEREWITH, REMAINS SOLELY WITH YOU, TO THE MAXIMUM EXTENT PERMITTED UNDER APPLICABLE LAW.

LIMITATION OF LIABILITY.

UBER SHALL NOT BE LIABLE FOR INDIRECT, INCIDENTAL, SPECIAL, EXEMPLARY, PUNITIVE, OR CONSEQUENTIAL DAMAGES, INCLUDING LOST PROFITS, LOST DATA, PERSONAL INJURY, OR PROPERTY DAMAGE RELATED TO, IN CONNECTION WITH, OR OTHERWISE RESULTING FROM ANY USE OF THE SERVICES, REGARDLESS OF THE NEGLIGENCE (EITHER ACTIVE, AFFIRMATIVE, SOLE, OR CONCURRENT) OF UBER, EVEN IF UBER HAS BEEN ADVISED OF THE POSSIBILITY OF SUCH DAMAGES.

UBER SHALL NOT BE LIABLE FOR ANY DAMAGES, LIABILITY OR LOSSES ARISING OUT OF: (i) YOUR USE OF OR RELIANCE ON THE SERVICES OR YOUR INABILITY TO ACCESS OR USE THE SERVICES; OR (ii) ANY TRANSACTION OR RELATIONSHIP BETWEEN YOU AND ANY THIRD PARTY PROVIDER, EVEN IF UBER HAS BEEN ADVISED OF THE POSSIBILITY OF SUCH DAMAGES. UBER SHALL NOT BE LIABLE FOR DELAY OR FAILURE IN PERFORMANCE RESULTING FROM CAUSES BEYOND UBER'S REASONABLE CONTROL. YOU ACKNOWLEDGE THAT THIRD PARTY PROVIDERS PROVIDING TRANSPORTATION SERVICES REQUESTED THROUGH SOME REQUEST PRODUCTS MAY OFFER RIDESHARING OR PEER-TO-PEER TRANSPORTATION SERVICES AND MAY NOT BE PROFESSIONALLY LICENSED OR PERMITTED.

THE SERVICES MAY BE USED BY YOU TO REQUEST AND SCHEDULE TRANSPORTATION, GOODS, OR LOGISTICS SERVICES WITH THIRD PARTY PROVIDERS, BUT YOU AGREE THAT UBER HAS NO RESPONSIBILITY OR LIABILITY TO YOU RELATED TO ANY TRANSPORTATION, GOODS OR LOGISTICS SERVICES PROVIDED TO YOU BY THIRD PARTY PROVIDERS OTHER THAN AS EXPRESSLY SET FORTH IN THESE TERMS.

THE LIMITATIONS AND DISCLAIMER IN THIS SECTION DO NOT PURPORT TO LIMIT LIABILITY OR ALTER YOUR RIGHTS AS A CONSUMER THAT CANNOT BE EXCLUDED UNDER APPLICABLE LAW. BECAUSE SOME STATES OR JURISDICTIONS DO NOT ALLOW THE EXCLUSION OF OR THE LIMITATION OF LIABILITY FOR CONSEQUENTIAL OR INCIDENTAL DAMAGES, IN SUCH STATES OR JURISDICTIONS, UBER'S LIABILITY SHALL BE LIMITED TO THE EXTENT PERMITTED BY LAW. THIS PROVISION SHALL HAVE NO EFFECT ON UBER'S CHOICE OF LAW PROVISION SET FORTH BELOW.

Indemnity.

You agree to indemnify and hold Uber and its affiliates and their officers, directors, employees, and agents harmless from any and all claims, demands, losses, liabilities, and expenses (including attorneys' fees), arising out of or in connection with: (i) your use of the Services or services or goods obtained through your use of the Services; (ii) your breach or violation of any of these Terms; (iii) Uber's use of your User Content; or (iv) your violation of the rights of any third party, including Third Party Providers.

7. Other Provisions

Choice of Law.

These Terms are governed by and construed in accordance with the laws of the State of California, U.S.A., without giving effect to any conflict of law principles, except as may be otherwise provided in the Arbitration Agreement above or in supplemental terms applicable to your region. However, the choice of law provision regarding the interpretation of these Terms is not intended to create any other substantive right to non-Californians to assert claims under California law whether that be by statute, common law, or otherwise. These provisions, and except as otherwise provided in Section 2 of these Terms, are only intended to specify the use of California law to interpret these Terms and the forum for disputes asserting a breach of these Terms, and these provisions shall not be interpreted as generally extending California law to you if you do not otherwise reside in California. The foregoing choice of law and forum selection provisions do not apply to the arbitration clause in Section 2 or to any arbitrable disputes as defined therein. Instead, as described in Section 2, the Federal Arbitration Act shall apply to any such disputes.

Claims of Copyright Infringement.

Claims of copyright infringement should be sent to Uber's designated agent. Please visit Uber's web page at https://www.uber.com/legal/intellectual-property/copyright/global for the designated address and additional information.

Notice.

Uber may give notice by means of a general notice on the Services, electronic mail to your email address in your Account, telephone or text message to any phone number provided in connection with your account, or by written communication sent by first class mail or pre-paid post to any address connected with your Account. Such notice shall be deemed to have been given upon the expiration of 48 hours after mailing or posting (if sent by first class mail or pre-paid post) or 12 hours after sending (if sent by email or telephone). You may give notice to Uber, with such notice deemed given when received by Uber, at any time by first class mail or pre-paid post to our registered agent for service of process, c/o Uber USA, LLC. The name and current contact information for the registered agent in each state are available online

General.

You may not assign these Terms without Uber's prior written approval. Uber may assign these Terms without your consent to: (i) a subsidiary or affiliate; (ii) an acquirer of Uber's equity, business or assets; or (iii) a successor by merger. Any purported assignment in violation of this section shall be void. No joint venture, partnership, employment, or agency relationship exists between you, Uber or any Third Party Provider as a result of this Agreement or use of the Services. If any provision of these Terms is held to be invalid or unenforceable, such provision shall be struck and the remaining provisions shall be enforced to the fullest extent under law. Uber's failure to enforce any right or provision in these Terms shall not constitute a waiver of such right or provision unless acknowledged and agreed to by Uber in writing. This provision shall not affect the Severability and Survivability section of the Arbitration Agreement of these Terms

Legal

Uber Copyright Policy

U.S. Only

Notification of Copyright Infringement:
Uber Technologies, Inc. ("Uber") respects the intellectual property rights of others and expects its users to do the same.

It is Uber's policy, in appropriate circumstances and at its discretion, to disable and/or terminate the accounts of users who repeatedly infringe or are repeatedly charged with infringing the copyrights or other intellectual property rights of others.

In accordance with the Digital Millennium Copyright Act of 1998, the text of which may be found on the U.S. Copyright Office website, Uber will respond expeditiously to claims of copyright infringement committed using the Uber website or other online network accessible through a mobile device or other type of device (the "Sites") that are reported to Uber's Designated Copyright Agent, identified in the sample notice below.

If you are a copyright owner, or are authorized to act on behalf of one, or authorized to act under any exclusive right under copyright, please report alleged copyright infringements taking place on or through the Sites by completing the following DMCA Notice of Alleged Infringement and delivering it to Uber's Designated Copyright Agent. Upon receipt of the Notice as described below, Uber will take whatever action, in its sole discretion, it deems appropriate, including removal of the challenged material from the Sites.

DMCA Notice of Alleged Infringement ("Notice")

1. *Identify the copyrighted work that you claim has been infringed, or - if multiple copyrighted works are covered by this Notice - you may provide a representative list of the copyrighted works that you claim have been infringed.*

2. *Identify the material that you claim is infringing (or to be the subject of infringing activity) and that is to be removed or access to which is to be disabled, and information reasonably sufficient to permit us to locate the material, including at a minimum, if applicable, the URL of the link shown on the Site(s) where such material may be found.*

3. *Provide your mailing address, telephone number, and, if available, email address.*

4. Include both of the following statements in the body of the Notice:

"I hereby state that I have a good faith belief that the disputed use of the copyrighted material is not authorized by the copyright owner, its agent, or the law (e.g., as a fair use)."

"I hereby state that the information in this Notice is accurate and, under penalty of perjury, that I am the owner, or authorized to act on behalf of the owner, of the copyright or of an exclusive right under the copyright that is allegedly infringed."

5. Provide your full legal name and your electronic or physical signature.

Deliver this Notice, with all items completed, to Uber's Designated Copyright Agent:

Copyright Agent

c/o Uber Technologies, Inc.

182 Howard Street # 8

San Francisco, CA 94105

dmca [at] uber [dot] com

IMPORTANT: Communications unrelated to copyright use or infringement will be discarded.

Please follow this link for Uber's Guidelines for Third Party Data Requests and Service of Legal Documents.

Lyft Terms of Service

Last Updated: February 6, 2018

These terms of service constitute a legally binding agreement (the "Agreement") between you and Lyft, Inc. ("Lyft," "we," "us" or "our") governing your use of the Lyft application, website, and technology platform (collectively, the "Lyft Platform").

Please be advised: This Agreement contains provisions that govern how claims you and Lyft have against each other can be brought (see Section 17 below). These provisions will, with limited exception, require you to submit claims you have against Lyft to binding and final arbitration on an individual basis, not as a plaintiff or class member in any class, group or representative action or proceeding. As a Driver or Driver applicant, you have an opportunity to opt out of arbitration with respect to certain claims as provided in Section 17.

By entering into to this Agreement, and/or by using or accessing the Lyft platform you expressly acknowledge that you understand this Agreement (including the dispute resolution and arbitration provisions in Section 17) and accept all of its terms. If you do not agree to be bound by the terms and conditions of this Agreement, you may not use or access the Lyft Platform. If you use the services of Lyft or its affiliates in another country, by using the Lyft Platform in that country you agree to be subject to Lyft's terms of service for that country.

The Lyft Platform

The Lyft Platform provides a marketplace where persons who seek transportation to certain destinations ("Riders") can be matched with persons driving to or through those destinations ("Drivers"). Drivers and Riders are collectively referred to herein as "Users," and each User shall create a User account that enables access to the Lyft Platform. Each person may only create one User account, and Lyft reserves the right to shut down any additional accounts. As a User, you authorize Lyft to match you with a Driver or Rider based on factors such as your location, the estimated time to pickup, your destination, user preferences, and platform efficiency, and to cancel an existing match and rematch based on the same considerations. For purposes of this Agreement, the driving services provided by Drivers to Riders that are matched through the Platform shall be referred to collectively as the "Services". Any decision by a User to offer or accept Services is a decision made in such User's sole discretion. Each transportation Service provided by a Driver to a Rider shall constitute a separate agreement between such persons.

Modification to the Agreement

In the event Lyft modifies the terms and conditions of this Agreement, such modifications shall be binding on you only upon your acceptance of the modified Agreement. Lyft reserves the right to modify any information referenced in the hyperlinks from this Agreement from time to time, and such modifications shall become effective upon posting. Continued use of the Lyft

Platform or Services after any such changes shall constitute your consent to such changes. Unless material changes are made to the arbitration provisions herein, you agree that modification of this Agreement does not create a renewed opportunity to opt out of arbitration (if applicable).

Eligibility

The Lyft Platform may only be used by individuals who can form legally binding contracts under applicable law. The Lyft Platform is not available to children (persons under the age of 18) or Users who have had their User account temporarily or permanently deactivated. By becoming a User, you represent and warrant that you are at least 18 years old and that you have the right, authority and capacity to enter into and abide by the terms and conditions of this Agreement. You may not allow other persons to use your User account, and you agree that you are the sole authorized user of your account.

Charges

As a Rider, you understand that request or use of the Services may result in charges to you ("Charges"). Charges include Fares and other applicable fees, tolls, surcharges, and taxes as set forth on your market's Lyft Cities page (www.lyft.com/cities), plus any tips to the Driver that you elect to pay. Lyft has the authority and reserves the right to determine and modify pricing by posting applicable pricing terms to your market's Lyft Cities page or quoting you a price for a specific ride at the time you make a request. Pricing may vary based on the type of service you request (e.g., Lyft Plus, Lyft SUV) as described on your market's Lyft Cities page. You are responsible for reviewing the applicable Lyft Cities page or price quote within the Lyft app and shall be responsible for all Charges incurred under your User account regardless of your awareness of such Charges or the amounts thereof.

Fares. There are two types of fares, variable and quoted.

- **Variable Fares.** Variable fares consist of a base charge and incremental charges based on the duration and distance of your ride. For particularly short rides, minimum fares may apply. Please note that we use GPS data from your Driver's phone to calculate the distance traveled on your ride. We cannot guarantee the availability or accuracy of GPS data. If we lose signal we will calculate time and distance using available data from your ride.
- **Quoted Fares.** In some cases Lyft may quote you a Fare at the time of your request. The quote is subject to change until the ride request is confirmed. If during your ride you change your destination, make multiple stops, or attempt to abuse the Lyft Platform, we may cancel the fare quote and charge you a variable fare based on the time and distance of your ride. Lyft does not guarantee that the quoted fare price will be equal to a variable fare for the same ride.

Fees and Other Charges.

- **Service Fee**. You may be charged a "Service Fee" for each ride as set forth on the applicable Lyft Cities page.
- **Prime Time**. At times of high demand for Services ("Prime Time") you acknowledge that Charges may increase substantially. For all rides with a variable fare, we will use reasonable efforts to inform you of any Prime Time multipliers in effect at the time of your request. For quoted fares we may factor in the Prime Time multiplier into the quoted price of the ride.
- **Cancellation Fee**. After requesting a ride you may cancel it through the app, but note that in certain cases a cancellation fee may apply. You may also be charged if you fail to show up after requesting a ride. Please check out our Help Center to learn more about Lyft's cancellation policy, including applicable fees.
- **Damage Fee**. If a Driver reports that you have materially damaged the Driver's vehicle, you agree to pay a "Damage Fee" of up to $250 depending on the extent of the damage (as determined by Lyft in its sole discretion), towards vehicle repair or cleaning. Lyft reserves the right (but is not obligated) to verify or otherwise require documentation of damages prior to processing the Damage Fee.
- **Tolls**. In some instances tolls (or return tolls) may apply to your ride. Please see our Help Center and your market's Lyft Cities page for more information about toll charges and a list of applicable tolls and return charges. We do not guarantee that the amount charged by Lyft will match the toll charged to the Driver, if any.
- **Other Charges**. Other fee and surcharges may apply to your ride, including: actual or anticipated airport fees, state or local fees, event fees as determined by Lyft or its marketing partners, and processing fees for split payments. In addition, where required by law Lyft will collect applicable taxes. See your market's Lyft Cities page for details on other Charges that may apply to your ride.
- **Tips**. Following a ride, you may elect to tip your Driver in cash or through the Lyft application. Any tips will be provided entirely to the applicable Driver.

General.

- **Facilitation of Charges**. All Charges are facilitated through a third-party payment processing service (e.g., Stripe, Inc., or Braintree, a division of PayPal, Inc.). Lyft may replace its third-party payment processing services without notice to you. Charges shall only be made through the Lyft Platform. With the exception of tips, cash payments are strictly prohibited. Your payment of Charges to Lyft satisfies your payment obligation for your use of the Lyft Platform and Services.
- **No Refunds**. All Charges are non-refundable. This no-refund policy shall apply at all times regardless of your decision to terminate usage of the Lyft Platform, any disruption to the Lyft Platform or Services, or any other reason whatsoever.
- **Coupons**. You may receive coupons that you can apply toward payment of certain Charges upon completion of a Ride. Coupons are only valid for use on the Lyft Platform, and are not transferable or redeemable for cash except as required by law. Coupons cannot be

combined, and if the cost of your ride exceeds the applicable credit or discount value we will charge your payment method on file for the outstanding cost of the Ride. For quoted or variable fares, Lyft may deduct the amount attributable to the Service Fee, Tolls, or Other Charges before application of the coupon. If you split payment for a Ride with another User, your coupon will only apply to your portion of the Charges. Additional restrictions on coupons may apply as communicated to you in a relevant promotion or by clicking on the relevant coupon within the Promotions section of the Lyft App.

- **Credit Card Authorization**. Upon addition of a new payment method or each ride request, Lyft may seek authorization of your selected payment method to verify the payment method, ensure the ride cost will be covered, and protect against unauthorized behavior. The authorization is not a charge, however, it may reduce your available credit by the authorization amount until your bank's next processing cycle. Should the amount of our authorization exceed the total funds on deposit in your account, you may be subject to overdraft of NSF charges by the bank issuing your debit or prepaid card. We cannot be held responsible for these charges and are unable to assist you in recovering them from your issuing bank. Check out our Help Center to learn more about our use of pre-authorization holds.

Payments

If you are a Driver, you will receive payment for your provision of Services pursuant to the terms of the Driver Addendum, which shall form part of this Agreement between you and Lyft. The Driver Addendum is available in the Driver dashboard when you log into your account.

Lyft Communications

By entering into this Agreement or using the Platform, you agree to receive communications from us, including via e-mail, text message, calls, and push notifications. You agree that texts, calls or prerecorded messages may be generated by automatic telephone dialing systems. Communications from Lyft, its affiliated companies and/or Drivers, may include but are not limited to: operational communications concerning your User account or use of the Lyft Platform or Services, updates concerning new and existing features on the Lyft Platform, communications concerning promotions run by us or our third-party partners, and news concerning Lyft and industry developments. Standard text messaging charges applied by your cell phone carrier will apply to text messages we send.

If you wish to opt out of promotional emails, you can unsubscribe from our promotional email list by following the unsubscribe options in the promotional email itself. If you wish to opt out of promotional calls or texts, you may text "END" to 46080 from the mobile device receiving the messages. You acknowledge that you are not required to consent to receive promotional texts or calls as a condition of using the Lyft Platform or the Services. If you wish to opt out of all texts or calls from Lyft (including operational or transactional texts or calls), you can text the word "STOPALL" to 46080 from the mobile device receiving the messages, however you acknowledge that opting out of receiving all texts may impact your use of the Lyft Platform or the Services.

Your Information

Your Information is any information you provide, publish or post to or through the Lyft Platform (including any profile information you provide) or send to other Users (including via in-application feedback, any email feature, or through any Lyft-related Facebook, Twitter or other social media posting) (your "Information"). You consent to us using your Information to create a User account that will allow you to use the Lyft Platform and participate in the Services. Our collection and use of personal information in connection with the Lyft Platform and Services is as provided in Lyft's Privacy Policy located at www.lyft.com/privacy. You are solely responsible for your Information and your interactions with other members of the public, and we act only as a passive conduit for your online posting of your Information. You agree to provide and maintain accurate, current and complete information and that we and other members of the public may rely on your Information as accurate, current and complete. To enable Lyft to use your Information for the purposes described in the Privacy Policy and this Agreement, you grant to us a non-exclusive, worldwide, perpetual, irrevocable, royalty-free, transferable, sub-licensable (through multiple tiers) right and license to exercise the copyright, publicity, and database rights you have in your Information, and to use, copy, perform, display and distribute such Information to prepare derivative works, or incorporate into other works, such Information, in any media now known or not currently known. Lyft does not assert any ownership over your Information; rather, as between you and Lyft, subject to the rights granted to us in this Agreement, you retain full ownership of all of your Information and any intellectual property rights or other proprietary rights associated with your Information.

You may be able to create or log-in to your Lyft User account through online accounts you may have with third party social networking sites (each such account, an "SNS Account"). By connecting to Lyft through an SNS Account, you understand that Lyft may access, store, and make available any SNS Account content according to the permission settings of your SNS Account (e.g., friends, mutual friends, contacts or following/followed lists (the "SNS Content")). You understand that SNS Content may be available on and through the Lyft Platform to other Users. Unless otherwise specified in this Agreement, all SNS Content, if any, shall be considered to be your Information.

Promotions and Referral Programs

Lyft, at its sole discretion, may make available promotions with different features to any Users or prospective Users. These promotions, unless made to you, shall have no bearing whatsoever on your Agreement or relationship with Lyft. Lyft reserves the right to withhold or deduct credits or benefits obtained through a promotion in the event that Lyft determines or believes that the redemption of the promotion or receipt of the credit or benefit was in error, fraudulent, illegal, or in violation of the applicable promotion terms or this Agreement.

As part of your User account, Lyft may provide you with or allow you to create a "Lyft Code," a unique alphanumeric code for you to distribute to your friends and family (each a "Referred User") to become new Lyft Riders ("Referred Riders") or Drivers ("Referred Drivers") in your country. Lyft Codes may only be distributed for promotional purposes and must be given away free of charge. You may not sell, trade, or barter your Lyft Code. You are prohibited from advertising Lyft Codes in any way, including through any of the following: Google, Facebook, Twitter, Bing and Craigslist. Lyft reserves the right to deactivate or invalidate any Lyft Code at any time in Lyft's discretion.

From time to time, Lyft may offer you with incentives to refer your friends and family to become new Users of the Lyft Platform in your country (the "Referral Program"). These incentives may come in the form of Lyft Credits, and Lyft may set or change the incentive types, amounts, terms, restrictions, and qualification requirements for any incentives in its sole discretion. Your distribution of Lyft Codes and participation in the Referral Program is subject to this Agreement and the additional Referral Program rules.

Restricted Activities

With respect to your use of the Lyft Platform and your participation in the Services, you agree that you will not:

1. impersonate any person or entity;
2. stalk, threaten, or otherwise harass any person, or carry any weapons;
3. violate any law, statute, rule, permit, ordinance or regulation;
4. interfere with or disrupt the Lyft Platform or the servers or networks connected to the Lyft Platform;
5. post Information or interact on the Lyft Platform or Services in a manner which is fraudulent, libelous, abusive, obscene, profane, sexually oriented, harassing, or illegal;
6. use the Lyft Platform in any way that infringes any third party's rights, including: intellectual property rights, copyright, patent, trademark, trade secret or other proprietary rights or rights of publicity or privacy;
7. post, email or otherwise transmit any malicious code, files or programs designed to interrupt, damage, destroy or limit the functionality of any computer software or hardware or telecommunications equipment or surreptitiously intercept or expropriate any system, data or personal information;
8. forge headers or otherwise manipulate identifiers in order to disguise the origin of any information transmitted through the Lyft Platform;
9. "frame" or "mirror" any part of the Lyft Platform, without our prior written authorization or use meta tags or code or other devices containing any reference to us in order to direct any person to any other web site for any purpose;
10. modify, adapt, translate, reverse engineer, decipher, decompile or otherwise disassemble any portion of the Lyft Platform or any software used on or for the Lyft Platform;
11. rent, lease, lend, sell, redistribute, license or sublicense the Lyft Platform or access to any portion of the Lyft Platform;

12. use any robot, spider, site search/retrieval application, or other manual or automatic device or process to retrieve, index, scrape, "data mine", or in any way reproduce or circumvent the navigational structure or presentation of the Lyft Platform or its contents;
13. link directly or indirectly to any other web sites;
14. transfer or sell your User account, password and/or identification to any other party
15. discriminate against or harass anyone on the basis of race, national origin, religion, gender, gender identity, physical or mental disability, medical condition, marital status, age or sexual orientation, or
16. cause any third party to engage in the restricted activities above.

Driver Representations, Warranties and Agreements

By providing Services as a Driver on the Lyft Platform, you represent, warrant, and agree that:

1. You possess a valid driver's license and are authorized and medically fit to operate a motor vehicle and have all appropriate licenses, approvals and authority to provide transportation to Riders in all jurisdictions in which you provide Services.
2. You own, or have the legal right to operate, the vehicle you use when providing Services, and such vehicle is in good operating condition and meets the industry safety standards and all applicable statutory and state department of motor vehicle requirements for a vehicle of its kind.
3. You will not engage in reckless behavior while driving, drive unsafely, operate a vehicle that is unsafe to drive, permit an unauthorized third party to accompany you in the vehicle while providing Services, provide Services as a Driver while under the influence of alcohol or drugs, or take action that harms or threatens to harm the safety of the Lyft community or third parties.
4. You will only provide Services using the vehicle that has been reported to, and approved by Lyft, and for which a photograph has been provided to Lyft, and you will not transport more passengers than can securely be seated in such vehicle (and no more than seven (7) passengers in any instance).
5. You will not, while providing the Services, operate as a public or common carrier or taxi service, accept street hails, charge for rides (except as expressly provided in this Agreement), demand that a rider pay in cash, or use a credit card reader, such as a Square Reader, to accept payment or engage in any other activity in a manner that is inconsistent with your obligations under this Agreement.
6. You will not attempt to defraud Lyft or Riders on the Lyft Platform or in connection with your provision of Services. If we suspect that you have engaged in fraudulent activity we may withhold applicable Fares or other payments for the ride(s) in question.
7. You will make reasonable accommodation for Riders and/or for service animals, as required by law and our Service Animal Policy.
8. You agree that we may obtain information about you, including your criminal and driving records, and you agree to provide any further necessary authorizations to facilitate our access to such records during the term of the Agreement.

9. You have a valid policy of liability insurance (in coverage amounts consistent with all applicable legal requirements) that names or schedules you for the operation of the vehicle you use to provide Services.
10. You will pay all applicable federal, state and local taxes based on your provision of Services and any payments received by you.

Intellectual Property

All intellectual property rights in the Lyft Platform shall be owned by Lyft absolutely and in their entirety. These rights include database rights, copyright, design rights (whether registered or unregistered), trademarks (whether registered or unregistered) and other similar rights wherever existing in the world together with the right to apply for protection of the same. All other trademarks, logos, service marks, company or product names set forth in the Lyft Platform are the property of their respective owners. You acknowledge and agree that any questions, comments, suggestions, ideas, feedback or other information ("Submissions") provided by you to us are non-confidential and shall become the sole property of Lyft. Lyft shall own exclusive rights, including all intellectual property rights, and shall be entitled to the unrestricted use and dissemination of these Submissions for any purpose, commercial or otherwise, without acknowledgment or compensation to you.

LYFT and other Lyft logos, designs, graphics, icons, scripts and service names are registered trademarks, trademarks or trade dress of Lyft in the United States and/or other countries (collectively, the "Lyft Marks"). If you provide Services as a Driver, Lyft grants to you, during the term of this Agreement, and subject to your compliance with the terms and conditions of this Agreement, a limited, revocable, non-exclusive license to display and use the Lyft Marks solely in connection with providing the Services through the Lyft Platform ("License"). The License is non-transferable and non-assignable, and you shall not grant to any third party any right, permission, license or sublicense with respect to any of the rights granted hereunder without Lyft's prior written permission, which it may withhold in its sole discretion. The Lyft Marks may not be used in any manner that is likely to cause confusion.

You acknowledge that Lyft is the owner and licensor of the Lyft Marks, including all goodwill associated therewith, and that your use of the Lyft Marks will confer no additional interest in or ownership of the Lyft Marks in you but rather inures to the benefit of Lyft. You agree to use the Lyft Marks strictly in accordance with Lyft's Trademark Usage Guidelines, as may be provided to you and revised from time to time, and to immediately cease any use that Lyft determines to nonconforming or otherwise unacceptable.

You agree that you will not: (1) create any materials that use the Lyft Marks or any derivatives of the Lyft Marks as a trademark, service mark, trade name or trade dress, other than as expressly approved by Lyft in writing; (2) use the Lyft Marks in any way that tends to impair their validity as proprietary trademarks, service marks, trade names or trade dress, or use the Lyft Marks other than in accordance with the terms, conditions and restrictions herein; (3) take any other action that would jeopardize or impair Lyft's rights as owner of the Lyft Marks or the legality and/or enforceability of the Lyft Marks, including, challenging or opposing Lyft's ownership in the Lyft Marks; (4) apply for trademark registration or renewal of trademark registration of any of the Lyft Marks, any derivative of the Lyft Marks, any combination of the Lyft Marks and any other name, or any trademark, service mark, trade name, symbol or word which is similar to the Lyft Marks; (5) use the Lyft Marks on or in connection with any product, service or activity that is in violation of any law, statute, government regulation or standard.

Violation of any provision of this License may result in immediate termination of the License, in Lyft's sole discretion. If you create any materials bearing the Lyft Marks (in violation of this Agreement or otherwise), you agree that upon their creation Lyft exclusively owns all right, title and interest in and to such materials, including any modifications to the Lyft Marks or derivative works based on the Lyft Marks. You further agree to assign any interest or right you may have in such materials to Lyft, and to provide information and execute any documents as reasonably requested by Lyft to enable Lyft to formalize such assignment.

Lyft respects the intellectual property of others, and expects Users to do the same. If you believe, in good faith, that any materials on the Lyft Platform or Services infringe upon your copyrights, please view our Copyright Policy for information on how to make a copyright complaint.

Disclaimers

The following disclaimers are made on behalf of Lyft, our affiliates, subsidiaries, parents, successors and assigns, and each of our respective officers, directors, employees, agents, and shareholders.

Lyft does not provide transportation services, and Lyft is not a transportation carrier. Lyft is not a common carrier or public carrier. It is up to the Driver to decide whether or not to offer a ride to a Rider contacted through the Lyft Platform, and it is up to the Rider to decide whether or not to accept a ride from any Driver contacted through the Lyft Platform. We cannot ensure that a Driver or Rider will complete an arranged transportation service. We have no control over the quality or safety of the transportation that occurs as a result of the Services.

The Lyft Platform is provided on an "as is" basis and without any warranty or condition, express, implied or statutory. We do not guarantee and do not promise any specific results from use of the Lyft Platform and/or the Services, including the ability to provide or receive Services at any given location or time. To the fullest extent permitted by law, we specifically disclaim any implied warranties of title, merchantability, fitness for a particular purpose and non-infringement. Some states do not allow the disclaimer of implied warranties, so the foregoing disclaimer may not apply to you.

We do not warrant that your use of the Lyft Platform or Services will be accurate, complete, reliable, current, secure, uninterrupted, always available, or error- free, or will meet your requirements, that any defects in the Lyft Platform will be corrected, or that the Lyft Platform is free of viruses or other harmful components. We disclaim liability for, and no warranty is made with respect to, connectivity and availability of the Lyft Platform or Services.

We cannot guarantee that each Rider is who he or she claims to be. Please use common sense when using the Lyft Platform and Services, including looking at the photos of the Driver or Rider you have matched with to make sure it is the same individual you see in person. Please note that there are also risks of dealing with underage persons or people acting under false pretense, and we do not accept responsibility or liability for any content, communication or other use or access of the Lyft Platform by persons under the age of 18 in violation of this Agreement. We encourage you to communicate directly with each potential Driver or Rider prior to engaging in an arranged transportation service.

Lyft is not responsible for the conduct, whether online or offline, of any User of the Lyft Platform or Services. You are solely responsible for your interactions with other Users. We do not procure insurance for, nor are we responsible for, personal belongings left in the car by Drivers or Riders. By using the Lyft Platform and participating in the Services, you agree to accept such risks and agree that Lyft is not responsible for the acts or omissions of Users on the Lyft Platform or participating in the Services.

You are responsible for the use of your User account and Lyft expressly disclaims any liability arising from the unauthorized use of your User account. Should you suspect that any unauthorized party may be using your User account or you suspect any other breach of security, you agree to notify us immediately.

It is possible for others to obtain information about you that you provide, publish or post to or through the Lyft Platform (including any profile information you provide), send to other Users, or share during the Services, and to use such information to harass or harm you. We are not responsible for the use of any personal information that you disclose to other Users on the Lyft Platform or through the Services. Please carefully select the type of information that you post on the Lyft Platform or through the Services or release to others. We disclaim all liability, regardless of the form of action, for the acts or omissions of other Users (including unauthorized users, or "hackers").

Opinions, advice, statements, offers, or other information or content concerning Lyft or made available through the Lyft Platform, but not directly by us, are those of their respective authors, and should not necessarily be relied upon. Such authors are solely responsible for such content. Under no circumstances will we be responsible for any loss or damage resulting from your reliance on information or other content posted by third parties, whether on the Lyft Platform or otherwise. We reserve the right, but we have no obligation, to monitor the materials posted on the Lyft Platform and remove any such material that in our sole opinion violates, or is alleged to violate, the law or this agreement or which might be offensive, illegal, or that might violate the rights, harm, or threaten the safety of Users or others.

Location data provided by the Lyft Platform is for basic location purposes only and is not intended to be relied upon in situations where precise location information is needed or where erroneous, inaccurate or incomplete location data may lead to death, personal injury, property or environmental damage. Neither Lyft, nor any of its content providers, guarantees the availability, accuracy, completeness, reliability, or timeliness of location data tracked or displayed by the Lyft Platform. Any of your Information, including geolocational data, you upload, provide, or post on the Lyft Platform may be accessible to Lyft and certain Users of the Lyft Platform.

Lyft advises you to use the Lyft Platform with a data plan with unlimited or very high data usage limits, and Lyft shall not responsible or liable for any fees, costs, or overage charges associated with any data plan you use to access the Lyft Platform.

This paragraph applies to any version of the Lyft Platform that you acquire from the Apple App Store. This Agreement is entered into between you and Lyft. Apple, Inc. ("Apple") is not a party to this Agreement and shall have no obligations with respect to the Lyft Platform. Lyft, not Apple, is solely responsible for the Lyft Platform and the content thereof as set forth hereunder. However, Apple and Apple's subsidiaries are third party beneficiaries of this Agreement. Upon your acceptance of this Agreement, Apple shall have the right (and will be deemed to have accepted the right) to enforce this Agreement against you as a third party beneficiary thereof. This Agreement incorporates by reference Apple's Licensed Application End User License Agreement, for purposes of which, you are "the end-user." In the event of a conflict in the terms of the Licensed Application End User License Agreement and this Agreement, the terms of this Agreement shall control.

As a Driver, you may be able to use "Lyft Nav built by Google" while providing Services on the Platform. If you elect to use this feature, you agree that Google may collect your location data when the Lyft App is running in order to provide and improve Google's services, that such data may also be shared with Lyft in order to improve its operations, and that Google's terms and privacy policy will apply to this usage.

State and Local Disclosures

Certain jurisdictions require additional disclosures to you. You can view any disclosures required by your local jurisdiction at www.lyft.com/terms/disclosures. We will update the disclosures page as jurisdictions add, remove or amend these required disclosures, so please check in regularly for updates.

Indemnity

You will defend, indemnify, and hold Lyft including our affiliates, subsidiaries, parents, successors and assigns, and each of our respective officers, directors, employees, agents, or shareholders harmless from any claims, actions, suits, losses, costs, liabilities and expenses (including reasonable attorneys' fees) relating to or arising out of your use of the Lyft Platform and participation in the Services, including: (1) your breach of this Agreement or the documents it incorporates by reference; (2) your violation of any law or the rights of a third party, including, Drivers, Riders, other motorists, and pedestrians, as a result of your own interaction with such third party; (3) any allegation that any materials that you submit to us or transmit through the Lyft Platform or to us infringe or otherwise violate the copyright, trademark, trade secret or other intellectual property or other rights of any third party; (4) your ownership, use or operation of a motor vehicle or passenger vehicle, including your provision of Services as a Driver; and/or (5) any other activities in connection with the Services. This indemnity shall be applicable without regard to the negligence of any party, including any indemnified person.

Limitation of Liability

In no event will Lyft, including our affiliates, subsidiaries, parents, successors and assigns, and each of our respective officers, directors, employees, agents, or shareholders (collectively "Lyft" for purposes of this section), be liable to you for any incidental, special, exemplary, punitive, consequential, or indirect damages (including damages for deletion, corruption, loss of data, loss of programs, failure to store any information or other content maintained or transmitted by the Lyft Platform, service interruptions, or for the cost of procurement of substitute services) arising out of or in connection with the Lyft Platform, the Services, or this Agreement, however arising including negligence, even if we or our agents or representatives know or have been advised of the possibility of such damages. The Lyft Platform may be used by you to request and schedule transportation, goods, or other services with third party providers, but you agree that Lyft has no responsibility or liability to you related to any transportation, goods or other services provided to you by third party providers other than as expressly set forth in this agreement. Certain jurisdictions may not allow the exclusion or limitation of certain damages. If these laws apply to you, some or all of the above disclaimers, exclusions or limitations may not apply to you, and you may have additional rights.

Term and Termination

This Agreement is effective upon your creation of a User account. This Agreement may be terminated: a) by User, without cause, upon seven (7) days' prior written notice to Lyft; or b) by either Party immediately, without notice, upon the other Party's material breach of this Agreement, including but not limited to any breach of Section 9 or breach of Section 10(a) through (i) of this Agreement. In addition, Lyft may terminate this Agreement or deactivate your User account immediately in the event: (1) you no longer qualify to provide Services or to operate the approved vehicle under applicable law, rule, permit, ordinance or regulation; (2) you fall below Lyft's star rating or cancellation threshold; (3) Lyft has the good faith belief that such action is necessary to protect the safety of the Lyft community or third parties, provided that in the event of a deactivation pursuant to (1)-(3) above, you will be given notice of the potential or actual deactivation and an opportunity to attempt to cure the issue to Lyft's reasonable satisfaction prior to Lyft permanently terminating the Agreement. For all other breaches of this Agreement, you will be provided notice and an opportunity to cure the breach. If the breach is cured in a timely manner and to Lyft's satisfaction, this Agreement will not be permanently terminated. Sections 2, 6, 7 (with respect to the license), 11-12, 14-19, and 21 shall survive any termination or expiration of this Agreement.

Dispute Resolution and Arbitration Agreement

(a) Agreement to Binding Arbitration Between You and Lyft.

You and Lyft mutually agree to waive our respective rights to resolution of disputes in a court of law by a judge or jury and agree to resolve any dispute by arbitration, as set forth below. This agreement to arbitrate ("Arbitration Agreement") is governed by the Federal Arbitration Act and survives after the Agreement terminates or your relationship with Lyft ends. Any arbitration under this Agreement will take place on an individual basis; class arbitrations and class actions are not permitted. Except as expressly provided below, this Arbitration Agreement applies to all Claims (defined below) between you and Lyft, including our affiliates, subsidiaries, parents, successors and assigns, and each of our respective officers, directors, employees, agents, or shareholders. This Arbitration Agreement also applies to claims between you and Lyft's service providers, including but not limited to background check providers and payment processors; and such service providers shall be considered intended third party beneficiaries of this Arbitration Agreement.

Except as expressly provided below, all disputes and claims between us (each a "Claim" and collectively, "Claims") shall be exclusively resolved by binding arbitration solely between you and Lyft. These Claims include, but are not limited to, any dispute, claim or controversy, whether based on past, present, or future events, arising out of or relating to: this Agreement and prior versions thereof (including the breach, termination, enforcement, interpretation or validity thereof), the Lyft Platform, the Services, any other goods or services made available through the Lyft Platform, your relationship with Lyft, the threatened or actual suspension, deactivation or termination of your User Account or this Agreement, background checks performed by or on Lyft's behalf, payments made by you or any payments made or allegedly owed to you, any promotions or offers made by Lyft, any city, county, state or federal wage-hour law, trade secrets, unfair competition, compensation, breaks and rest periods, expense reimbursement, wrongful termination, discrimination, harassment, retaliation, fraud, defamation, emotional distress, breach of any express or implied contract or covenant, claims arising under federal or state consumer protection laws; claims arising under antitrust laws, claims arising under the Telephone Consumer Protection Act and Fair Credit Reporting Act; and claims arising under the Uniform Trade Secrets Act, Civil Rights Act of 1964, Americans With Disabilities Act, Age Discrimination in Employment Act, Older Workers Benefit Protection Act, Family Medical Leave Act, Fair Labor Standards Act, Employee Retirement Income Security Act (except for individual claims for employee benefits under any benefit plan sponsored by Lyft and covered by the Employee Retirement Income Security Act of 1974 or funded by insurance), and state statutes, if any, addressing the same or similar subject matters, and all other federal and state statutory and common law claims. All disputes concerning the arbitrability of a Claim (including disputes about the scope, applicability, enforceability, revocability or validity of the Arbitration Agreement) shall be decided by the arbitrator, except as expressly provided below.

By agreeing to arbitration, you understand that you and Lyft are waiving the right to sue in court or have a jury trial for all Claims, except as expressly otherwise provided in this Arbitration Agreement. This Arbitration Agreement is intended to require arbitration of every claim or dispute that can lawfully be arbitrated, except for those claims and disputes which by the terms of this Arbitration Agreement are expressly excluded from the requirement to arbitrate.

(b) Prohibition of Class Actions and Non-Individualized Relief.

You understand and agree that you and Lyft may each bring Claims in arbitration against the other only in an individual capacity and not on a class, collective action, or representative basis ("Class Action Waiver"). You understand and agree that you and Lyft both are waiving the right to pursue or have a dispute resolved as a plaintiff or class member in any purported class, collective or representative proceeding. Notwithstanding the foregoing, this subsection (b) shall not apply to representative private attorneys general act claims brought against Lyft, which are addressed separately in Section 17(c).

The arbitrator shall have no authority to consider or resolve any Claim or issue any relief on any basis other than an individual basis. The arbitrator shall have no authority to consider or resolve any Claim or issue any relief on a class, collective, or representative basis. The arbitrator may award declaratory or injunctive relief only in favor of the individual party seeking relief and only to the extent necessary to provide relief warranted by that party's individual claims.

Notwithstanding any other provision of this Agreement, the Arbitration Agreement or the AAA Rules, disputes regarding the scope, applicability, enforceability, revocability or validity of the Class Action Waiver may be resolved only by a civil court of competent jurisdiction and not by an arbitrator. In any case in which: (1) the dispute is filed as a class, collective, or representative action and (2) there is a final judicial determination that the Class Action Waiver is unenforceable as to any Claims, then those Claims shall be severed from any remaining claims and may be brought in a civil court of competent jurisdiction, but the Class Action Waiver shall be enforced in arbitration on an individual basis as to all other Claims to the fullest extent possible.

(c) Representative PAGA Waiver.

Notwithstanding any other provision of this Agreement or the Arbitration Agreement, to the fullest extent permitted by law: (1) you and Lyft agree not to bring a representative action on behalf of others under the Private Attorneys General Act of 2004 ("PAGA"), California Labor Code § 2698 et seq., in any court or in arbitration, and (2) for any claim brought on a private attorney general basis, including under the California PAGA, both you and Lyft agree that any such dispute shall be resolved in arbitration on an individual basis only (i.e., to resolve whether you have personally been aggrieved or subject to any violations of law), and that such an action may not be used to resolve the claims or rights of other individuals in a single or collective proceeding (i.e., to resolve whether other individuals have been aggrieved or subject to any violations of law) (collectively, "representative PAGA Waiver"). Notwithstanding any other provision of this Agreement, the Arbitration Agreement or the AAA Rules, disputes regarding the scope, applicability, enforceability, revocability or validity of this representative PAGA Waiver may be resolved only by a civil court of competent jurisdiction and not by an arbitrator. If any provision of this representative PAGA Waiver is found to be unenforceable or unlawful for any reason: (i) the unenforceable provision shall be severed from this Agreement; (ii) severance of the unenforceable provision shall have no impact whatsoever on the Arbitration Agreement or the requirement that any remaining Claims be arbitrated on an individual basis pursuant to the Arbitration Agreement; and (iii) any such representative PAGA or other representative private attorneys general act claims must be litigated in a civil court of competent jurisdiction and not in arbitration. To the extent that there are any Claims to be litigated in a civil court of competent jurisdiction because a civil court of competent jurisdiction determines that the representative PAGA Waiver is unenforceable with respect to those Claims, the Parties agree that litigation of those Claims shall be stayed pending the outcome of any individual Claims in arbitration.

(d) Rules Governing the Arbitration.

Any arbitration conducted pursuant to this Arbitration Agreement shall be administered by the American Arbitration Association ("AAA") pursuant to its Consumer Arbitration Rules that are in effect at the time the arbitration is initiated, as modified by the terms set forth in this Agreement. Copies of these rules can be obtained at the AAA's website (www.adr.org) (the "AAA Rules") or by calling the AAA at 1-800-778-7879. Notwithstanding the foregoing, if requested by you and if proper based on the facts and circumstances of the Claims presented, the arbitrator shall have the discretion to select a different set of AAA Rules, but in no event shall the arbitrator consolidate more than one person's Claims, or otherwise preside over any form of representative, collective, or class proceeding.

As part of the arbitration, both you and Lyft will have the opportunity for reasonable discovery of non-privileged information that is relevant to the Claim. The arbitrator may award any individualized remedies that would be available in court. The arbitrator may award declaratory or injunctive relief only in favor of the individual party seeking relief and only to the extent necessary to provide relief warranted by that party's individual claims. The arbitrator will provide a reasoned written statement of the arbitrator's decision which shall explain the award given and the findings and conclusions on which the decision is based.

The arbitrator will decide the substance of all claims in accordance with applicable law, and will honor all claims of privilege recognized by law. The arbitrator shall not be bound by rulings in prior arbitrations involving different Riders or Drivers, but is bound by rulings in prior arbitrations involving the same Rider or Driver to the extent required by applicable law. The arbitrator's award shall be final and binding and judgment on the award rendered by the arbitrator may be entered in any court having jurisdiction thereof, provided that any award may be challenged in a court of competent jurisdiction.

(e) Arbitration Fees and Awards.

The payment of filing and arbitration fees will be governed by the relevant AAA Rules subject to the following modifications:

1. If you initiate arbitration under this Arbitration Agreement after participating in the optional Negotiation process described in subsection (k) below and are otherwise required to pay a filing fee under the relevant AAA Rules, Lyft agrees that, unless your claim is for $5,000 or more, your share of the filing and arbitration fees is limited to $50, and that, after you submit proof of payment of the filing fee to Lyft, Lyft will promptly reimburse you for all but $50 of the filing fee. If, however, the arbitrator finds that either the substance of your claim or the relief sought in the claim is frivolous or brought for an improper purpose (as measured by the standards set forth in Federal Rule of Civil Procedure 11(b)), then the payment of all such fees will be governed by the AAA Rules.
2. If Lyft initiates arbitration under this Arbitration Agreement, Lyft will pay all AAA filing and arbitration fees.
3. With respect to any Claims brought by Lyft against a Driver, or for Claims brought by a Driver against Lyft that: (A) are based on an alleged employment relationship between Lyft and a Driver; (B) arise out of, or relate to, Lyft's actual deactivation of a Driver's User account or a threat by Lyft to deactivate a Driver's User account; (C) arise out of, or relate to, Lyft's actual termination of a Driver's Agreement with Lyft under the termination provisions of this Agreement, or a threat by Lyft to terminate a Driver's Agreement; (D) arise out of, or relate to, Fares (as defined in this Agreement, including Lyft's commission or fees on the Fares), tips, or average hourly guarantees owed by Lyft to Drivers for Services, other than disputes relating to referral bonuses, other Lyft promotions, or consumer-type disputes, or (E) arise out of or relate to background checks performed in connection with a user seeking to become a Driver (the subset of Claims in subsections (A)-(E) shall be collectively referred to as "Driver Claims"), Lyft shall pay all costs unique to arbitration (as compared to the costs of adjudicating the same claims before a court), including the regular and customary arbitration fees and expenses (to the extent not paid by Lyft pursuant to the fee provisions above). However, if you are the party initiating the Driver Claim, you shall be responsible for contributing up to an amount equal to the filing fee that would be paid to initiate the claim in the court of general jurisdiction in the state in which you provide Services to Riders, unless a lower fee amount would be owed by you pursuant to the AAA Rules, applicable law, or subsection (e)(1) above. Any dispute as to whether a cost is unique to arbitration shall be resolved by the arbitrator. For purposes of this Section 17(e)(3), the term "Driver" shall be deemed to include both Drivers and Driver applicants who have not been approved to drive.
4. Except as provided in Federal Rule of Civil Procedure 68 or any state equivalents, each party shall pay its own attorneys' fees and pay any costs that are not unique to the

arbitration (i.e., costs that each party would incur if the claim(s) were litigated in a court such as costs to subpoena witnesses and/or documents, take depositions and purchase deposition transcripts, copy documents, etc.).
5. At the end of any arbitration, the arbitrator may award reasonable fees and costs or any portion thereof to you if you prevail, to the extent authorized by applicable law.
6. Although under some laws Lyft may have a right to an award of attorneys' fees and non-filing fee expenses if it prevails in an arbitration, Lyft agrees that it will not seek such an award.
7. If the arbitrator issues you an award that is greater than the value of Lyft's last written settlement offer made after you participated in good faith in the optional Negotiation process described in subsection (k) below, then Lyft will pay you the amount of the award or U.S. $1,000, whichever is greater.

(f) Location and Manner of Arbitration.

Unless you and Lyft agree otherwise, any arbitration hearings between Lyft and a Rider will take place in the county of your billing address, and any arbitration hearings between Lyft and a Driver will take place in the county in which the Driver provides Services. If AAA arbitration is unavailable in your county, the arbitration hearings will take place in the nearest available location for a AAA arbitration. If your Claim is for $10,000 or less, Lyft agrees that you may choose whether the arbitration will be conducted solely on the basis of documents submitted to the arbitrator, through a telephonic hearing, or by an in-person hearing as determined by the AAA Rules. If your Claim exceeds $10,000, the right to a hearing will be determined by the AAA Rules.

(g) Exceptions to Arbitration.

This Arbitration Agreement shall not require arbitration of the following types of claims: (1) small claims actions brought on an individual basis that are within the scope of such small claims court's jurisdiction; (2) a representative action brought on behalf of others under PAGA or other private attorneys general acts, to the extent the representative PAGA Waiver in Section 17(c) of such action is deemed unenforceable by a court of competent jurisdiction under applicable law not preempted by the FAA; (3) claims for workers' compensation, state disability insurance and unemployment insurance benefits; and (4) claims that may not be subject to arbitration as a matter of generally applicable law not preempted by the FAA.

Nothing in this Arbitration Agreement prevents you from making a report to or filing a claim or charge with the Equal Employment Opportunity Commission, U.S. Department of Labor, Securities Exchange Commission, National Labor Relations Board ("NLRB"), or Office of Federal Contract Compliance Programs, or similar local, state or federal agency, and nothing in this Arbitration Agreement shall be deemed to preclude or excuse a party from bringing an administrative claim before any agency in order to fulfill the party's obligation to exhaust administrative remedies before making a claim in arbitration However, should you bring an administrative claim, you may only seek or recover money damages of any type pursuant to this

Arbitration Provision, and you knowingly and voluntarily waive the right to seek or recover money damages of any type pursuant to any administrative complaint, except for a complaint issued by the NLRB. Should you participate in an NLRB proceeding, you may only recover money damages if such recovery does not arise from or relate to a claim previously adjudicated under this Arbitration Provision or settled by you. Similarly, you may not recover money damages under this Arbitration Provision if you have already adjudicated such claim with the NLRB. Nothing in this Agreement or Arbitration Agreement prevents your participation in an investigation by a government agency of any report, claim or charge otherwise covered by this Arbitration Provision.

(h) Severability.

In addition to the severability provisions in subsections (c) above, in the event that any portion of this Arbitration Agreement is deemed illegal or unenforceable under applicable law not preempted by the FAA, such provision shall be severed and the remainder of the Arbitration Agreement shall be given full force and effect.

(i) Driver Claims in Pending Settlement.

If you are a member of a putative class in a lawsuit against Lyft involving Driver Claims and a Motion for Preliminary Approval of a Settlement has been filed with the court in that lawsuit prior to this Agreement's effective date (a "Pending Settlement Action"), then this Arbitration Agreement shall not apply to your Driver Claims in that particular class action. Instead, your Driver Claims in that Pending Settlement Action shall continue to be governed by the arbitration provisions contained in the applicable Agreement that you accepted prior to this Agreement's effective date.

(j) Opting Out of Arbitration for Driver Claims That Are Not In a Pending Settlement Action.

As a Driver or Driver applicant, you may opt out of the requirement to arbitrate Driver Claims defined in Section 17(e)(3) (except as limited by Section 17(i) above) pursuant to the terms of this subsection if you have not previously agreed to an arbitration provision in Lyft's Terms of Service where you had the opportunity to opt out of the requirement to arbitrate. If you have previously agreed to such an arbitration provision, you may opt out of any revisions to your prior arbitration agreement made by this provision in the manner specified below, but opting out of this arbitration provision has no effect on any previous, other, or future arbitration agreements that you may have with Lyft. If you have not previously agreed to such an arbitration provision and do not wish to be subject to this Arbitration Agreement with respect to Driver Claims, you may opt out of arbitration with respect to such Driver Claims, other than those in a Pending Settlement Action, by notifying Lyft in writing of your desire to opt out of arbitration for such Driver Claims, which writing must be dated, signed and delivered by: (1) electronic mail to arbitrationoptout@lyft.com, or (2) by certified mail, postage prepaid and return receipt requested, or by any nationally recognized delivery service (e.g, UPS, Federal Express, etc.) that is addressed to:

General Counsel
Lyft, Inc.
185 Berry St., Suite 5000
San Francisco, CA 94107

In order to be effective, (A) the writing must clearly indicate your intent to opt out of this Arbitration Agreement with respect to Driver Claims that are not part of a Pending Settlement Action, (B) the writing must include the name, phone number, and email address associated with your User Account, and (C) the email or envelope containing the signed writing must be sent within 30 days of the date this Agreement is executed by you. Should you not opt out within the 30-day period, you and Lyft shall be bound by the terms of this Arbitration Agreement in full (including with respect to Driver Claims that are not part of a Pending Settlement Action). As provided in paragraph 17(i) above, any opt out that you submit shall not apply to any Driver Claims that are part of a Pending Settlement Action and your Driver Claims in any such Pending Settlement Action shall continue to be governed by the arbitration provisions that are contained in the applicable Lyft Terms of Use that you agreed to prior to the effective date of this Agreement.

Cases have been filed against Lyft and may be filed in the future involving Driver Claims. You should assume that there are now, and may be in the future, lawsuits against Lyft alleging class, collective, and/or representative Driver Claims in which the plaintiffs seek to act on your behalf, and which, if successful, could result in some monetary recovery to you. But if you do agree to arbitration of Driver Claims with Lyft under this Arbitration Agreement, you are agreeing in advance that you will bring all such claims, and seek all monetary and other relief, against Lyft in an individual arbitration provision, except for the Driver Claims that are part of a Pending Settlement Action. You are also agreeing in advance that you will not participate in, or seek to recover monetary or other relief, for such claims in any court action or class, collective, and/or representative action. You have the right to consult with counsel of your choice concerning this Arbitration Agreement and you will not be subject to retaliation if you exercise your right to assert claims or opt- out of any Driver Claims under this Arbitration Agreement.

(k) Optional Pre-Arbitration Negotiation Process.

Before initiating any arbitration or proceeding, you and Lyft may agree to first attempt to negotiate any dispute, claim or controversy between the parties informally for 30 days, unless this time period is mutually extended by you and Lyft. A party who intends to seek negotiation under this subsection must first send to the other a written notice of the dispute ("Notice"). The Notice must (1) describe the nature and basis of the claim or dispute; and (2) set forth the specific relief sought. All offers, promises, conduct and statements, whether oral or written, made in the course of the negotiation by any of the parties, their agents, employees, and attorneys are confidential, privileged and inadmissible for any purpose, including as evidence of liability or for impeachment, in arbitration or other proceeding involving the parties, provided that evidence that is otherwise admissible or discoverable shall not be rendered inadmissible or non-discoverable as a result of its use in the negotiation.

Confidentiality

You agree not to use any technical, financial, strategic and other proprietary and confidential information relating to Lyft's business, operations and properties, information about a User made available to you in connection with such User's use of the Platform, which may include the User's name, pick-up location, contact information and photo ("Confidential Information") disclosed to you by Lyft for your own use or for any purpose other than as contemplated herein. You shall not disclose or permit disclosure of any Confidential Information to third parties. You agree to take all reasonable measures to protect the secrecy of and avoid disclosure or use of Confidential Information of Lyft in order to prevent it from falling into the public domain. Notwithstanding the above, you shall not have liability to Lyft with regard to any Confidential Information which you can prove: was in the public domain at the time it was disclosed by Lyft or has entered the public domain through no fault of yours; was known to you, without restriction, at the time of disclosure, as demonstrated by files in existence at the time of disclosure; is disclosed with the prior written approval of Lyft; becomes known to you, without restriction, from a source other than Lyft without breach of this Agreement by you and otherwise not in violation of Lyft's rights; or is disclosed pursuant to the order or requirement of a court, administrative agency, or other governmental body; provided, however, that You shall provide prompt notice of such court order or requirement to Lyft to enable Lyft to seek a protective order or otherwise prevent or restrict such disclosure.

Relationship with Lyft

As a Driver on the Lyft Platform, you acknowledge and agree that you and Lyft are in a direct business relationship, and the relationship between the parties under this Agreement is solely that of independent contracting parties. You and Lyft expressly agree that (1) this is not an employment agreement and does not create an employment relationship between you and Lyft; and (2) no joint venture, franchisor- franchisee, partnership, or agency relationship is intended or created by this Agreement. You have no authority to bind Lyft, and you undertake not to hold yourself out as an employee, agent or authorized representative of Lyft.

Lyft does not, and shall not be deemed to, direct or control you generally or in your performance under this Agreement specifically, including in connection with your provision of Services, your acts or omissions, or your operation and maintenance of your vehicle. You retain the sole right to determine when, where, and for how long you will utilize the Lyft Platform. You retain the option to accept or to decline or ignore a Rider's request for Services via the Lyft Platform, or to cancel an accepted request for Services via the Lyft Platform, subject to Lyft's then-current cancellation policies. With the exception of any signage required by law or permit/license rules or requirements, Lyft shall have no right to require you to: (a) display Lyft's names, logos or colors on your vehicle(s); or (b) wear a uniform or any other clothing displaying Lyft's names, logos or colors. You acknowledge and agree that you have complete discretion to provide Services or otherwise engage in other business or employment activities.

Other Services

In addition to connecting Riders with Drivers, the Lyft Platform may enable Users to provide or receive goods or services from other third parties. For example, Users may be able to use the Lyft Platform to order a delivery of goods, purchase a digital item, request a carpool ride from a commuter going in your direction, or when travelling outside of the United States, to connect with local transportation platforms and request rides from local drivers (collectively, the "Other Services"). You understand and that the Other Services are subject to the terms and pricing of the third-party provider. If you choose to purchase Other Services through the Lyft Platform, you authorize Lyft to charge your payment method on file according to the pricing terms set by the third-party provider. You agree that Lyft is not responsible and may not be held liable for the Other Services or the actions or omissions of the third- party provider. Such Other Services may not be investigated, monitored or checked for accuracy, appropriateness, or completeness by us, and we are not responsible for any Other Services accessed through the Lyft Platform.

General

Except as provided in Section 17, this Agreement shall be governed by the laws of the State of California without regard to choose of law principles. This choice of law provision is only intended to specify the use of California law to interpret this Agreement and is not intended to create any other substantive right to non- Californians to assert claims under California law whether by statute, common law, or otherwise. If any provision of this Agreement is or becomes invalid or non- binding, the parties shall remain bound by all other provisions of this Agreement. In that event, the parties shall replace the invalid or non-binding provision with provisions that are valid and binding and that have, to the greatest extent possible, a similar effect as the invalid or non-binding provision, given the contents and purpose of this Agreement. You agree that this Agreement and all incorporated agreements may be automatically assigned by Lyft, in our sole discretion by providing notice to you. Except as explicitly stated otherwise, any notices to Lyft shall be given by certified mail, postage prepaid and return receipt requested to Lyft, Inc., 185 Berry St., Suite 5000, San Francisco, CA 94107. Any notices to you shall be provided to you through the Lyft Platform or given to you via the email address or physical you provide to Lyft during the registration process. Headings are for reference purposes only and in no way define, limit, construe or describe the scope or extent of such section. The words "include", "includes" and "including" are deemed to be followed by the words "without limitation". A party's failure to act with respect to a breach by the other party does not constitute a waiver of the party's right to act with respect to subsequent or similar breaches. This Agreement sets forth the entire understanding and agreement between you and Lyft with respect to the subject matter hereof and supersedes all previous understandings and agreements between the parties, whether oral or written.

If you have any questions regarding the Lyft Platform or Services, please contact our Customer Support Team through our Help Center.

Lyft Privacy Policy

Last Updated: February 8, 2017

At Lyft, we want to connect people through transportation and bring communities together. In this privacy policy, we tell you what information we receive from Lyft riders and drivers, and how we use it to connect riders with drivers and continue to improve our services. Below, we explain how you can share with other riders and drivers in the Lyft community as part of our mission to bring people together.

Scope of this Privacy Policy

Lyft ("Lyft," "we," "our," and/or "us") values the privacy of individuals who use our application, websites, and related services (collectively, the "Lyft Platform "). This privacy policy (the "Privacy Policy") explains how we collect, use, and share information from Lyft users ("Users"), comprised of both Lyft riders ("Riders") and Lyft drivers (including Driver applicants) ("Drivers"). Beyond the Privacy Policy, your use of Lyft is also subject to our Terms of Service (www.lyft.com/terms).

Information We Collect

A. Information You Provide to Us

Registration Information. When you sign up for a Lyft account, you give us your name, email address, and phone number. If you decide to sign up for Lyft using your Facebook account, we will also get basic information from your Facebook profile like your name, gender, profile photo, and Facebook friends.

User Profile Information. When you join the Lyft community, you can create a Lyft Profile to share fun facts about yourself, and discover mutual friends and interests. Filling out a profile is optional, and you can share as little or as much as you want. Your name (and for Drivers, Profile photos) is always part of your Profile. Read more below about how you can control who sees your Profile. You can also add a Business Profile to your account, which requires a designated business email address and payment method.

Payment Method. When you add a credit card or payment method to your Lyft account, a third party that handles payments for us will receive your card information. To keep your financial data secure, we do not store full credit card information on our servers.

Communications. If you contact us directly, we may receive additional information about you. For example, when you contact our Customer Support Team, we will receive your name, email address, phone number, the contents of a message or attachments that you may send to us, and other information you choose to provide.

Driver Application Information. If you decide to join our Lyft driver community, in addition to the basic registration information we ask you for your date of birth, physical address, Social Security number, driver's license information, vehicle information, car insurance information, and in some jurisdictions we may collect additional business license or permitting information. We share this information with our partners who help us by running background checks on Drivers to help protect the Lyft community.

Payment Information. To make sure Drivers get paid, we keep information about Drivers' bank routing numbers, tax information, and any other payment information provided by Drivers.

B. Information We Collect When You Use the Lyft Platform

Location Information. Lyft is all about connecting Drivers and Riders. To do this, we need to know where you are. When you open Lyft on your mobile device, we receive your location. We may also collect the precise location of your device when the app is running in the foreground or background. If you label certain locations, such as "home" and "work," we receive that information, too.

Your location information is necessary for things like matching Riders with nearby Drivers, determining drop off and pick up locations, and suggesting destinations based on previous trips. Also, if the need ever arises, our Trust & Safety team may use and share location information to help protect the safety of Lyft Users or a member of the public. In addition to the reasons described above, Drivers' location information and distance travelled is necessary for calculating charges and insurance for Lyft rides. If you give us permission through your device settings or Lyft app, we may collect your location while the app is off to identify promotions or service updates in your area.

Device Information. Lyft receives information from Users' devices, including IP address, web browser type, mobile operating system version, phone carrier and manufacturer, application installations, device identifiers, mobile advertising identifiers, push notification tokens, and, if you register with your Facebook account, your Facebook identifier. We collect mobile sensor data from Drivers' devices (such as speed, direction, height, acceleration or deceleration) to improve location accuracy and analyze usage patterns.

Usage Information. To help us understand how you use the Lyft Platform and to help us improve it, we automatically receive information about your interactions with the Lyft Platform, like the pages or other content you view, your actions within the Lyft app, and the dates and times of your visits.

Call and Text Information. We work with a third party partner to facilitate phone calls and text messages between Riders and Drivers who have been connected for a ride. We receive information about these communications including the date and time of the call or SMS message, the parties' phone numbers, and the content of any SMS messages. For security purposes, we may also monitor and/or record the contents of phone calls made on the Lyft Platform, such as those between Riders and Drivers. You will be given notice that your call may be recorded, and by proceeding you agree to allow Lyft to monitor and/or record your call.

User Feedback. At Lyft, we want to make sure Users are always enjoying great rides. Riders and Drivers may rate and review each other at the end of every ride. We receive information about ratings and reviews and, as we explain below, give Riders information about Drivers' ratings and reviews and vice versa.

Address Book Contacts. If you permit Lyft to access the address book on your device through the permission system used by your mobile platform, we may access and store names and contact information from your address book to facilitate invitations and social interactions that you initiate through our Platform and for other purposes described in this privacy policy or at the time of consent or collection.

Information from Cookies and Similar Technologies. We collect information through the use of "cookies", tracking pixels, and similar technologies to understand how you navigate through the Lyft Platform and interact with Lyft advertisements, to learn what content is popular, and to save your preferences. Cookies are small text files that web servers place on your device; they are designed to store basic information and to help websites and apps recognize your browser. We may use both session cookies and persistent cookies. A session cookie disappears after you close your browser. A persistent cookie remains after you close your browser and may be accessed every time you use the Lyft Platform. You should consult your web browser(s) to modify your cookie settings. Please note that if you delete or choose not to accept cookies from us, you may be missing out on certain features of the Lyft Platform.

C. Information We Collect from Third Parties

Third Party Services. If you choose to register for Lyft or otherwise link your Lyft account with a third party's service (such as Facebook), we may receive the same type of information we collect from you (described above) directly from those services.

Third Party Partners. We may receive additional information about you, such as demographic data, payment information, or fraud detection information, from third party partners and combine it with other information that we have about you.

Enterprise Programs. If your company, university, or organization participates in one of our enterprise programs such as Lyft for Work, we may receive information about you, such as your email address, from your participating organization. We also may give your participating organization the opportunity to request a ride on your behalf, in which case they may provide us with your name, phone number, and the pickup and drop off location for your ride.

Background Information on Drivers. Lyft works with third party partners to perform driving record and criminal background checks on Drivers, and we receive information from them such as publicly available information about a Driver's driving record or criminal history.

How We Use the Information We Collect

We use the information we collect from all Users to:

- Connect Riders with Drivers;
- Provide, improve, expand, and promote the Lyft Platform;
- Analyze how the Lyft community uses the Lyft Platform;
- Communicate with you, either directly or through one of our partners, including for marketing and promotional purposes;
- Personalize the Lyft experience for you and your friends and contacts;
- Send you text messages and push notifications;
- Facilitate transactions and payments;
- Provide you with customer support;
- Find and prevent fraud; and
- Respond to trust and safety issues that may arise, including auto incidents, disputes between Riders and Drivers, and requests from government authorities.

Additionally, we use the information we collect from Drivers for the following purposes related to driving on the Lyft Platform:

- Sending emails and text messages to Drivers who have started the driver application process regarding the status of their application;
- Determining a Driver's eligibility to drive for Lyft
- Notifying Drivers about ride demand, pricing and service updates; and
- Calculating and providing Lyft's auto insurance policy and analyzing usage patterns for safety and insurance purposes.

How We Share the Information We Collect

A. Sharing Between Users

Sharing between Riders and Drivers. Riders and Drivers that have been matched for a ride are able to see basic information about each other, such as names, photo, ratings, and any information they have added to their Profiles. Riders and Drivers who connect their Lyft accounts to Facebook will also be able to see their mutual Facebook friends during the ride. Drivers see the pick-up location that the Rider has provided. Riders see a Driver's vehicle information and real-time location as the Driver approaches the pick-up location. Riders' ratings of Drivers are shared with Drivers on a weekly basis. We de-identify the ratings and feedback, but we can't rule out that a driver may be able to identify the Rider that provided the rating or feedback.

Although we help Riders and Drivers communicate with one another to arrange a pickup, we do not share your actual phone number or other contact information with other Users. If you report a lost or found item to us, we will seek to connect you with the relevant Rider or Driver, including sharing actual contact information with your permission.

Sharing between Lyft Line Riders. If you use Lyft Line, Riders who have been matched with you will be able to see your name, photo and any information you have added to your Profile. If you connect your Lyft account to Facebook (such as by signing up through Facebook), we may show your mutual friends with other Riders who are also connected via Facebook. During the Lyft Line matching process we may show photos of possible matches to you and other Riders.

B. Sharing Between Lyft and Third Parties

API and Integration Partners. If you connect to the Lyft Platform through an integration with a third party service, we may share information about your use of the Lyft Platform with that third party. We may share your information with our third party partners in order to receive additional information about you. We may also share your information with third party partners to create offers that may be of interest to you.

Third Party Services. The Lyft Platform may allow you to connect with other websites, products, or services that we don't have control over (for example, we may give you the ability to order a food delivery from a restaurant from within the Lyft app). If you use these services, we will provide the third party with information about you to allow them to provide the service to you (for example, we would give the restaurant your name, phone number and address to drop off the food). We can't speak to the privacy practices of these third parties, and we encourage you to read their privacy policies before deciding whether to use their services.

Service Providers. We work with third party service providers to perform services on our behalf, and we may share your information with such service providers to help us provide the Lyft Platform, including all of the things described in Section 3 above.

Enterprise Partners. If you participate in an enterprise program and charge a ride to your organization's billing method or credits, we will provide your organization's account holder with information about your use of the Lyft Platform, including ride details such as date, time, charge, and pick up and drop off locations. If you create a Business Profile, at the end of each ride you will have the option to designate the ride as a business ride. If you do so, and your organization has a corporate account with Lyft, we may share information about your use of Lyft Platform with your organization including ride details such as date, time, charge, and region of the trip. If you change organizations, it is your responsibility to update your Business Profile with the new information. (Please remember to check and set your designation settings accordingly.) If you integrate your account with an expense platform (like Concur) we will share the ride details to your expense account.

International Partners. We've partnered with several ride-sharing services around the globe so Riders can continue to find rides when they open the Lyft app abroad, and Drivers can provide services to international travelers in the U.S. When we match a ride with the partner, we share the same information that is shared between matched Riders and Drivers on the Lyft Platform. In some cases we are unable to mask your phone number if you call an international driver, so please keep that in mind before using this feature.

Other Sharing. We may share your information with third parties in the following cases:

- While negotiating or in relation to a change of corporate control such as a restructuring, merger or sale of our assets;
- If a government authority requests information and we think disclosure is required or appropriate in order to comply with laws, regulations, or a legal process;
- With law enforcement officials, government authorities, or third parties if we think doing so is necessary to protect the rights, property, or safety of the Lyft community, Lyft, or the public (you can read more about this in our Law Enforcement Request policy);
- To comply with a legal requirement or process, including but not limited to, civil and criminal subpoenas, court orders or other compulsory disclosures.
- If you signed up for a promotion with another User's referral or promotion code, with your referrer to let them know about your redemption of or qualification for the promotion;
- With our insurance partners to help determine and provide relevant coverage in the event of an incident;
- To provide information about the use of the Lyft Platform to potential business partners in aggregated or de-identified form that can't reasonably be used to identify you; and
- Whenever you consent to the sharing.

Your Choices

Email Subscriptions. You can always unsubscribe from our commercial or promotional emails but we will still send you transactional and relational emails about your account use of the Lyft Platform.

Text Messages. You can opt out of receiving commercial or promotional text messages by texting the word END to 46080 from the mobile device receiving the messages. You may also opt out of receiving all texts from Lyft (including transactional or relational messages) by texting the word STOPALL to 46080 from the mobile device receiving the messages, however, opting out of receiving all texts may impact your use of the Lyft Platform. Drivers can also opt out of driver-specific messages by texting STOP in response to a driver SMS. To re-enable texts you can text START in response to an unsubscribe confirmation SMS.

Push Notifications. You can opt out of receiving push notifications through your device settings. Please note that opting out of receiving push notifications may impact your use of the Lyft Platform (such as receiving a notification that your ride has arrived).

Profile Information. While your name will always be shared with Drivers and fellow Lyft Line Riders, you can delete any additional information that you added to your Profile at any time if you don't want Drivers and Lyft Line Riders to see it. Riders will always be able to see Drivers' names, rating, profile photos, and vehicle information.

Location Information. While you can prevent your device from sharing location information at any time through your Device's operating system settings, Rider and Driver location is core to the Lyft Platform and without it we can't provide our services to you.

Facebook Friends. You can control whether to enable or disable the Facebook mutual friends feature through your profile settings.

Editing and Accessing Your Information. You can review and edit certain account information by logging in to your account settings and profile (Drivers may edit additional information through the Driver portal). If would like to terminate your Lyft account, please contact us through our Help Center with your request. If you choose to terminate your account, we will deactivate it for you but may retain information from your account for a certain period of time and disclose it in a manner consistent with our practices under this Privacy Policy for accounts that are not closed. We also may retain information from your account to collect any fees owed, resolve disputes, troubleshoot problems, analyze usage of the Lyft Platform, assist with any investigations, prevent fraud, enforce our Terms of Service, or take other actions as required or permitted by law.

Other

Data Security. We are committed to protecting the data of the Lyft community. Even though we take reasonable precautions to protect your data, no security measures can be 100% secure, and we cannot guarantee the security of your data.

Children's Privacy. Lyft is not directed to children, and we don't knowingly collect personal information from children under 13. If we find out that a child under 13 has given us personal information, we will take steps to delete that information. If you believe that a child under the age of 13 has given us personal information, please contact us at our Help Center.

Changes to Our Privacy Policy. We may make changes to this Privacy Policy from time to time. If we make any material changes, we will let you know through the Lyft Platform, by email, or other communication. We encourage you to read this Privacy Policy periodically to stay up-to-date about our privacy practices. As long as you use the Lyft Platform, you are agreeing to this Privacy Policy and any updates we make to it.

Contact Information. Feel free to contact us at any time with any questions or comments about this Privacy Policy, your personal information, our use and sharing practices, or your consent choices by contacting our Help Center.

Bibliography

https://www.nasdaq.com/article/who-are-ubers-biggest-competitors-cm860923
https://www.uber.com/
https://www.lyft.com/
https://www.ranker.com/list/rideshare-horror-stories/casey-cavanagh
https://ride.guru/content/newsroom/uber-driver-scams
https://www.rd.com/advice/travel/uber-scams-you-need-to-watch-out-for/
https://therideshareguy.com/the-scam-passengers-are-still-using/
https://maximumridesharingprofits.com/how-uber-and-lyft-drivers-get-scammed-by-passengers/